D1010681

NORTH VANCOUVER
DISTRICT LIBRARY

A Dublin Girl

A Dublin Girl

Growing Up in the 1930s

Elaine Crowley

SOHO

NORTH VANCOUVER
DISTRICT LIBRARY

First published in Ireland by The Lilliput Press Limited

Copyright © 1996 by Elaine Crowley; first published in
the United States of America in 1998

All rights reserved.

Published by
Soho Press, Inc.
853 Broadway
New York, NY 10003

Library of Congress Cataloging-in-Publication Data

Crowley, Elaine, 1927–
   [Cowslips and chainies]
   A Dublin girl : growing up in the 1930's / Elaine
Crowley.
      p.   cm.
   Originally published: Cowslips and chainies. Dublin :
Lilliput Press. 1996.
   ISBN 1-56947-112-6 (alk. paper)
   1. Crowley, Elaine, 1927– —Biography. 2. Novelists,
Irish—20th century—Biography. I. Title.
PR6053.R656Z464   1998
823' .914—dc21
[B]   97-18924
                                   CIP

10 9 8 7 6 5 4 3 2 1

ONE

A motorway is to be built on the street where I lived. The street to which I was brought home from the hospital where I was born. The house in which I lived is knocked down to the ground floor. The windows of the shop over which we had our accommodation are covered with sheets of corrugated iron. There are gaps where they meet. I can see in. See the piles of rubble, shards of planks that was the floor on which I played, plaster and layers of wallpaper, stained, faded, rotting, clinging to the bricks. Wallpaper my mother would have bought as 'end of line', at a knock-down price. Wallpaper that long ago came untrimmed. So that the inch-wide plain margins on each roll had to be cut away. Sometimes I was allowed to do this while my mother made flour and water paste. The margins fell in long, long curly streamers with which I festooned my head, transforming the straight-fringed brown bob into a mass of ringlets, and imagined I was Shirley Temple.

Amongst the rubble I spy a grate, rusted and pitted. I claim it as ours—it might have belonged to the other tenant who lived in the house. But, no, it's ours. I convince myself of that. Around it grow chickweed, groundsel and mauve convolvulus whose tendrils are entwined in the grate's bars.

Peering through the chink in the corrugated sheets I see my mother kneeling before the grate. Sheets of newspaper cover the lino. On them are laid soft cloths, black leading brushes and—in an orange and black striped paper package which has a picture of a zebra on its front—the polish.

I watch my mother open the cake of polish, spit on it, dip in a cloth, work it over the surface, and then, with her strong, square hands begin applying the polish. Laying down the cloth in favour of the smallest brush which will reach the corners and crevices of the grate, she sits back on her hunkers while waiting for the polish to dry, humming, talking aloud. Reminding herself of messages she has to do. Casting a glance at the window to judge if the weather will hold. Will the clothes dry. Will the baby sleep for another hour.

The polish dries. She wields the bigger brush and continues talking, now to me. She says, 'My father used to keep birds. Cages of them in the yard. Linnets, larks and canaries. I used to gather the chickweed and groundsel for them. Groundsel's the grand thing for feeding birds.' A dull gleam is coming to the grate's bars.

I saw a yard full of birds. I saw yellow canaries and heard the birds singing.

'Where did he get the birds?' I ask.

'In the Bird Market in Bride Street. Though sometimes he caught them. It's easy to catch birds. All you have to do is put salt on their tails.'

Her knuckles rasped on a bar, the skin breaking. She dropped the brush and sucked the blood from the broken skin.

'Mammy, can we do it, can we, Mammy?'

'Do what?' she asked, her voice full of irritation.

'Go down to the yard. I'll get the salt and we'll catch the birds. Can we, please Mammy?'

'Will you stop moidering me. Go on away and play. Go down and see if the baby's alright.'

The birds had flown like her thoughts. They were somewhere else now. Wondering if my father would come home late. Would St Jude answer her prayers. Would her ambitions be fulfilled.

My mother had two ambitions. To be on the pig's back and to have a private house. Now and then the arrival of American dollars from relations fulfilled for a while her first ambition. With the windfall, small debts to the corner shop were cleared. Articles of clothing, wedding presents, whatever she had pawned and was now in danger of running out of pledges would be released. Another source of unexpected income came from the numerous actions against Dublin Corporation when she fell off her high-heels on a broken path or got a touch of food poisoning from bad food, which, after the shopkeeper's refusal to refund her money, she took to the City Analyst. And great was her joy when her debts were cleared and a small sum was left over for her indulgence in antiques.

2

She had, she said, the eye for recognizing old beautiful things, and from her foraging in the second-hand markets she would return with her finds. Unwrapping and displaying exquisite wax-faced dolls, minus one or two limbs; miniature pewter tea-sets; hand-painted plates, once broken but repaired with metal stitches; pairs of horses she believed to be bronze, rearing on their inflexible reins. The plates were dusted, washed and put on shelves; the pair of horses on the mantlepiece; the doll promised to me, once it was mended; the pewter tea-set displayed on the sideboard. And if they were in season, the bags of soft fruit she had bought during her sojourn in the markets, which along with the antiques also sold old clothes, fish and soft fruits, were shared between me and my brother.

Her second ambition, she admitted, might take a long time to realize. Unless someone died and left her a fortune or she won the Irish Sweepstakes, for which she never in any case bought a ticket, a private house was aiming very high. Being practical as well as permanently hopeful, she put her name down for a Corporation place. But as she often said, 'There's families of ten and twelve children all over the city of Dublin being reared in one room and me with a fine airy room and only three children. It'll be years before I come anywhere near the top of the list. And if it wasn't for the hall door always open and anyone from the street free to use the lavatory, I'd stay where I am. Corporation schemes would never be my first choice.'

She also had great faith and so had enlisted the patron saint of hopeless causes, St Jude, to put in a word for her. 'And in any case,' she'd say when the dollars were spent, the amount from the small action gone, the pair of horses discovered to be gunmetal and not bronze, the doll gone to the dolls' hospital where it would remain an undischarged patient until the next windfall, 'Haven't I the future to look forward to. One day, please God, you'll all be grown up and earning, and then with your father's money as well, I'll have my own little house and be on the pig's back for the rest of my life.'

The room we lived in was over a shop that sold only salt. Salt that was delivered in enormous blocks before being crushed down and packed into cardboard boxes and sold to small shopkeepers who sold it on for a penny a packet. The room was large with two sash windows. There were alcoves on each side of the fireplace. In one there was a gas stove and in the other, behind a cretonne curtain, our clothes hung from nails. There was a double bed and a single one in which I slept with my brother. The baby's pram was also used as her cot. Our food was prepared and eaten from a long, narrow mahogany table with a bockaddy* leg which had to be propped with a wedge of cardboard. 'But,' my mother frequently proclaimed, 'it's a beautiful piece of wood. Look at the colour of it. None of your deal there'.

Her preference for the old table, the green plush horse-hair-stuffed chairs and enormous oak sideboard wasn't all a matter of taste. My father had refused to sign for anything on 'the weekly'. My mother argued that everyone had homes like palaces for five shillings a week. But my father was adamant—nothing on instalments.

'Feck him,' my mother's sister said when she heard of his refusal. 'If he won't provide you with a home get one behind his back. I know a fella that'll let on to be your husband. For five shillings he'd put his name to anything.'

So down to the Cavendish went my mother and the forger, and ordered the best cork-inlaid linoleum in a red Turkish pattern, a double bed, a modern sideboard and two leatherette armchairs. She said not a word to my father about the transaction, convinced that once the items were delivered he'd be so overwhelmed by their beauty and the transformation of the room nothing would be forthcoming except showers of praise. I was spellbound by the new furniture. Its brightness and newness. The smell of it. The smoothness of the oilcloth when I ran my hand along the roll, the coolness of it against my cheek. With the bed came a gift of two plump feather pillows in black and white ticking, soft and downy, yielding to the lightest pressure of my hands.

My mother called a boy from the street to help her take the old bed down to the yard and hoosh the spring onto the shed roof.

'It'll be out of the way there and I'll tie a line from one end to the drainpipe,' she said and gave the boy a shilling for his help. Singing at the top of her voice she came back to the room to arrange the furniture. She moved everything to one end of

---

* From the Irish word *bacach*, a person with a short leg.

the room and laid the first roll of linoleum, reversed the process and laid the other, assembled the bed, laid the table for tea and waited for my father to come home and shower her with praise.

Instead there was murder. My father shouting. My mother closing down the window so that the neighbours couldn't hear the row. Shouting in her turn. Telling him if he had provided her with a decent home there would have been no need for any deception. He threatened to have the furniture repossessed, refused his tea and went out. My mother went round the room, shifting delft and plates of food distractedly and talking to herself and answering my questions by telling me to shut up and not be driving her mad. A van came to collect the furniture.

'What about the bed and the oilcloth?' my mother asked the van driver.

'It sez here a sideboard and two chairs, that's all,' the man said. From behind the lace hangings she watched him load the van and knew that everyone else in the street was watching too.

'The dirty louser,' she kept saying. 'My own husband to do a thing like that on me. To make a show of me. I'll never forgive him, never.'

'To deprive you of the few sticks! That shows what he's made of,' her sister said when she discovered what had happened. By this time my mother and father had made it up. Their quarrels, though often bitter, seldom lasted long. And when they were friends she wouldn't hear a word against him. 'He did what was right. Bloody robbers, that's what them places are. Selling matchwood and charging you through the nose for it. He's getting a loan on Saturday and will buy me my wants.' My aunt persisted in criticizing my father. She and my mother had a row and each vowed never to darken the other's door again. That evening my mother confided to my father that it was all that wan's fault. If it hadn't been for her advice she would never have gone to the furniture shop. And in future she'd tell her less of her business. The oilcloth and the bed were never repossessed nor payment demanded. 'I could have told you that,' my aunt said, her quarrel with my mother made up. 'In the interest of hygiene they never take back beds. Sure they could have been pissed on or infected with bugs. And as for the oilcloth, once it's been laid it's never the same again. So you got something out of it. The new sideboard's nice. A lovely bit of oak and the carving's beautiful.'

'Wait'll I show you. Look at the way the drawers open. Lions' heads and you put your hand under their mouths.' My mother demonstrated proudly.

'All the same it's a bit on the big side for the room I'd say.' My mother said nothing but after her sister went told me that jealousy was all that ailed that wan. Mad jealous of the sideboard that was an antique. I didn't know what jealousy meant. But I knew my aunt was gorgeous and that I loved her. She laughed a lot and wore gold earrings and always answered my questions. And sometimes she wore a black leather coat, boots and helmet when she rode on the back of her husband's motorbike. And she promised that when I was a big girl I could ride on the bike. For a long time after the second lot of furniture was bought my mother was in constant good humour. Every day she polished the sideboard and enthused about the carving. The room smelled of Mansion Polish and the oak gleamed. While she polished she sang and I listened enthralled to her beautiful voice, memorizing the words, occasionally venturing to sing with her. A venture quickly quashed: 'You'll never make a singer. Listen and maybe you'll learn to carry an air,' she said and continued her song.

Along with the second-hand furniture, she had bought two large pictures in ornate gilt frames, one of 'Our Lady of Good Counsel' which hung above the double bed and one of 'Bubbles' for over mine. His green velvet suit was exactly the colour I would have liked for a dress. And his hair was beautiful. For days after the pictures came I would spit on my finger and try unsuccessfully to wind my straight heavy brown hair into little curls.

We now had three pictures in the room. The third, which had always been there, was of a woman in a long white dress which fell in folds on her bare feet. In her long dark hair she wore a wreath of flowers and held up high a branch of blossom. She was the most enchanting person I had ever seen and I believed for many years that the picture was of my mother when she was young. My mother said my father was a picture. I didn't understand that. She also sometimes said he was a whore-master and had a fancy woman. I didn't understand that either. But as I wasn't supposed to be listening to the conversation between her and my aunt I couldn't ask for an explanation. 'Don't be listening to what I'm talking about,' she frequently warned me,

6

but as there was nowhere else to go, for I wasn't yet allowed down into the street, I listened. Sometimes I forgot her warning and not only listened but asked questions to which her reply was, 'You be quiet. You're far too knowing for your age.'

My father, on the nights he stayed in, seldom spoke of things I didn't understand and when he did, he never minded my questions. He taught me poems, repeating the words until I knew them by heart. Sometimes I dreamed I was Lucy Grey lost in the snow, or the Skipper's daughter lashed to the mast of the Hesperus. I'd waken from my nightmares crying. He'd lift me from the bed, and safe in his arms I didn't mind my mother scolding, while she mixed cocoa and sugar for my drink, that he had me ruined.

My father worked for an undertaker. He earned two pounds ten shillings a week and sometimes made half as much again in tips. 'The poor', he said, 'are the best tippers.'

'God help them,' my mother would say. 'Gone mad with the society money. The only time in their lives when they have the handling of a few shillings.'

Like the rent-man, the society-man called every week. There were policies on my mother's and father's lives at fourpence each and policies on the childrens' for a penny a week. It was as important to pay the insurance as it was to pay the rent. Eviction was dreaded and so was a pauper's funeral. The dead must be given a good send-off. Several of my mother's neighbours didn't agree with this. One, I remember, often argued with her. 'I don't give a shite what they do with me when I'm dead. And one thing's sure and certain, I'm paying out no society money so that when I'm stretched stiff from the navel up and down the neighbours can say, "Look at the coffin. Solid oak. And look at the handles! God isn't she getting a great send-off." I'd like me job.'

'That's all very well,' my mother would reply, 'but who'll pay for your funeral? Who'll bury you? Answer me that.'

'If they don't bury me for pride, they'll bury me for stink,' the neighbour would say, and laugh loudly.

My father drove a hearse. Sometimes with two horses, sometimes, if there was a lot of society money, there were four horses. Black horses with plumes and a black velvet cloth covering their backs. The hearse driver wore a livery, a double-breasted black coat and a velour top-hat. I loved brushing my

7

father's hat. First one way so that the surface gleamed like satin and then against the grain so that the shine disappeared and the surface was rough.

Glass shades filled with plaster flowers, doves and crosses were the wreaths bought by the majority of people for the deceased. They were piled on the coffins and later on the graves. My mother was contemptuous of them. When she sent a wreath she bought fresh flowers and with wire and ribbon made her own. Chrysanthemums, bronze and yellow, come to mind, so her friends must have died when it was autumn. Yet all these years afterwards I still associate the smell of chrysanthemums with death.

On Sunday mornings my father took me with him to stable his horses. Dressed in my best and holding his hand we'd set off for the undertaker's yard in Denzille Street. Through William's Place past the back entrance of the Meath Hospital, through York Street where women sat on the steps of the tenement houses breastfeeding their babies, talking, laughing and shouting to their barefooted children playing in the road. Then out of the poverty-ridden street and onto the Green where all was sunshine and the women were pretty and wore beautiful clothes and from the gratings of the Shelbourne rose smells of delicious food. On through other streets where no women sat on the steps and the letter-boxes and knockers gleamed like gold.

'We're nearly there now,' my father would say as we turned into Lincoln Place. And we'd stop to look into the window where a poster showed pictures of tortured animals and my father explained that some doctors did cruel things for the sake of curing sick people. He didn't think that was any excuse and he had signed a petition against vivisection.

The yard smelled of hay and horses. Pigeons perched on the roofs of out-buildings waiting until I stood still before flying down to peck hayseeds from between the cobbles. For a while I'd watch my father mucking out. Afterwards I'd feed Dolly and Peggy the penny-bars of Savoy chocolate I'd bought for them. Then begin my exploring. Into the harness room touching belly-bands and bits, carriage lamps and halters. Moving onto the shed where the broughams and landaus were, and the brake, which sometimes on a summer's day my father drove to our street, filled with children and took them for a ride. In the carriage shed the hearses and mourning coaches were polished and ready for

8

the funerals on Monday morning. And beside them the box-shaped, windowless coffin-cart used for delivering the coffins to the home of the dead person and for burying the Jews.

I left exploring the coffin-shop until last, always hoping that by the time I reached there my father's whistle would signal that he had finished stabling and was ready to leave. I didn't want to go in and yet could not resist doing so. In I went, one part of my mind praying for the summons to go, and another side of me wanting to walk through the oak shavings. I loved the way they crunched beneath my feet like the fallen leaves in the park, and the smell of wood. There were always a few coffins finished, lined with white satin, and pillows to match, and the coffins' lids had writing on the brass plates.

If the weather was fine we went to the zoo. I bought peanuts from the dealers to feed the monkeys. My father showed me how to squeeze the ends of the nuts' shells. They split enough for me to wear them as earrings. On other Sundays we went to the Botanical Gardens. I didn't like them very much. They were too warm and the plants too big. I liked the National Art Gallery but not as much as the Natural History Museum. All the stuffed animals and the enormous Irish elk.

Lately, before setting off on our trips, we went to the cigarette shop across the road from the undertaker's yard. There was a girl serving—her name was Kathleen. She had black hair, short and straight and very shiny, and a fringe like mine. She gave me bars of chocolate, Fry's Cream and packets of Half-Time-Jimmy which had a picture of boys playing football on the wrapper. On the way home my father warned me to say nothing about the chocolate, otherwise my mother would fight with him for ruining my appetite.

TWO

'You can go down and play but don't go away from the door,' my mother instructed me the first time I was allowed into the street on my own. 'And don't go near the road,' she called after me. The road was the only danger she could envisage, for the road wasn't the street. The street was the people who lived there. She knew every one of them and they knew I was her little girl.

Sand lorries, on their way to and from the quarries in Rathfarnham, came down the road at great speed. An occasional motor car passed by. But mostly the traffic was horse-drawn. Big shire-horses pulled the Guinness drays to the public-houses. Coalmen and milkmen and Kennedy's and Johnston, Mooney and O'Brien bakers' vans delivered trays of steaming hot loaves and turnovers to the small shops. Funerals drove past on their way to Mount Jerome, going there at a modest pace, racing on the return journey.

Unless I went onto the road I was in no danger. Except those I imagined and was unable to communicate. Afraid of the dwarf who waddled past in her button boots. Her head and face were enormous, coarse hair sprouted profusely from her chin. She was so deformed, I'd heard my mother say, because she was born on the night of the big wind. And I imagined her as a new baby being rolled along the ground before the fierce wind, becoming more crumpled and misshapen the way newspapers did in the gutters. Afraid of the hunch-backed woman riding an ass and cart, collecting slops for her pigs. She had small pink-rimmed eyes that resembled those of the pigs she kept. They stared at my fat legs. And I remembered how my mother said pigs were scavengers and would eat anything.

I could acknowledge my terror of the cows on their way to

the slaughterhouse. Everyone was frightened of the fear-crazed animals. It was alright to comment on their wild staring eyes and lowered heads as they ran from side to side of the street, attempting to evade the blows rained on their backs by the drovers' blackthorn sticks and seek sanctuary from the fate they instinctively knew awaited them. I sat on the step and watched the world go by. Listened to the grown-ups talking, threatening to kill, murder, split or dye someone's eye. Sometimes threats were directed to me by an older child. But I soon learned that mostly it was all talk. The only one who raised a hand to you was your mother or father and God help anyone else who attempted to.

Passing women going for their messages, clutching a purse in one hand and a marketing bag in the other, gave me pennies or ha'pennies, smiled and told me I was getting a big girl. They were concerned for my comfort and safety and behaviour, urging me to go in if it began to rain, telling me not to go near the road, nor climb the railings or dirty my dress. Occasionally one might tell me off, and I'd tell my mother. 'Mrs so-and-so told me not to bounce my ball near her door.'

'I hope she didn't have to speak to you twice and that you didn't answer back,' was the standard reply if she liked the woman. If on the other hand my mother considered her 'a cranky oul' get' or a newcomer—a newcomer being anyone who hadn't been born in the street and her mother and father before her—she'd say, 'It wasn't today or yesterday the Foxes came into the street. Your feet are treading the stones I trod as a child. You play where you like. And wait till the next time I see that oul' wan.'

I was given permission to move away from the doorstep to play by degrees. I made friends, especially with Hannah, and formed likes and dislikes. One day Hannah and I sat on the curb making heaps of the summer dust that collected in the gutter, and planning to murder John Joe. John Joe was three and a half and I hated him. He was small for his age and had a pale face. The front of his trousers was always wet and he kept kicking over our carefully made mounds of dust.

'After we murder him, we'll chop him up in bits,' I explained to Hannah and she agreed with me.

A big dray went past on its way to Fitz's. Great dollops of steaming manure fell onto the road and the bluebottles appeared as if by magic. John Joe was forgotten as Hannah and I found two sticks and up-ended the shiny brown balls from which pieces of undigested bran poked. The disturbed flies went away. A passing woman shouted, 'Get off the road this minute before I tell your mother.'

'Let's go and watch the barrels,' I suggested.

Hannah said, 'All right,' and we followed the dray to the pub. John Joe started whingeing to come with us but I wouldn't let him. The grating was up and the men in aprons were already lowering the barrels into the cellar. It was very dark down there. Thick dust, like dirty grey wool, and sweet papers, clung to the sides of the walls. The smell of last night's porter was everywhere.

'Mind outta the way youse. Do you want to be kilt? Go on away and play,' one of the men in the apron roared. We moved off for new adventures.

'Let's go down the alley,' I said. The alley was a narrow lane which ran along the back of our side of the street. The shopkeepers threw their rubbish there. Sometimes there were damaged apples and oranges only slightly mouldy. And once I had found half-a-crown and my mother was delighted.

'I'll get into trouble if I go in the alley again,' Hannah said.

'Aw, come on. Only for a few minutes. Sure your mammy won't know,' I coaxed.

'No. I can't. Me mammy says I stink of fish when I've been in the alley.'

'We'll, I'm going. And if you tell I'll scrawb your eyes out.' I ran off and left her.

The alley was cool and dark. Battered dustbins overflowed and it smelled of fruit and rotten fish. I poked about looking for something or anything. A half empty vinegar bottle lay on its side amongst a patch of stinging nettles. I picked it up, pulled out the cork and drank it. I loved the sharp taste. My mother said you shouldn't drink vinegar, it dried up your blood. I didn't care. I drained the bottle and flung it over the wall.

Half way down the alley was a hill, a very small one. I climbed up and sat on the top. Pee-the-beds grew there and, nestling amongst the yellow flowers and ginny joe seed heads—that you could tell the time with by how many breaths it took to blow away the seeds—was a dead fish. The skin was coarse and dry. I turned it over with my foot. The underside was moist. I poked a stick through, breaking the skin, and saw thick white maggots wriggling. It looked like a moving rice pudding.

Hannah had changed her mind. I could see her now, timidly walking down the lane, stepping over the rotting vegetables. I hooked the stick inside the fish and flung it towards her. Clumps of maggots flew through the air. The fish missed her, hit the wall and landed on her white runners. She started to cry. 'I'll tell my mammy so I will. I won't play with you any more.' She ran sobbing through the alley.

On top of my hill I danced and chanted, 'Cry baby. Cry baby.' I was sorry when she went, and stopped singing. But after dinner we would make it up. I'd send someone to ask if she was 'spin spout, or black out'. If she said 'spin spout' we were friends. But if the answer was 'black out', I'd have to try again.

I climbed down the hill and started for home. I walked along the curb, my eyes down looking for treasure. Two seagull feathers lay on the tarry road. I dashed into the road and picked them up. Now I could play Indians after dinner. As I neared the hall door, John Joe sidled up. I stuck the feathers in my hair and did a war dance. He stared at me, his eyes vacant, pale and bulging like gooseberries. I stuck my tongue out and raced up the stairs. My mother was at the gas-stove cooking the dinner. 'Where have you been? And what's that you've got in your hair?' she asked looking around. 'I've been calling you for your dinner. I've never met such a child in my life. You're never where you should be. Where were you?' She didn't expect an answer so I kept quiet. I went to the window to watch for my father who would be home in a minute. I moved the lace hangings to get a better view.

'What's that you have in your hair? Take it out immediately.'

'Only two feathers. I was playing Indians.'

'I'll give you Indians. Take them out I said.'

I raised my hand and pulled the feathers. They fell forward over my face, the quills bending, but the ends remained firmly stuck in my hair. 'Will you take them things out of your hair? You've been down that alley. Look at the cut of you. And wash your hands, they're like pigs' paws. Take them out. How many more times do I have to tell you?' she shouted.

I tried again, pulling hard, wincing at the pain in my scalp. My mother crossed the room, looked at my hair and hit me a stinging slap. 'Sweet Jesus, look at your hair! It's full of tar!' A smell of burning filled the room. The drained potatoes, left over the flame to dry, had caught. She ran back to the cooker removing the pot and still giving out about my hair. 'What am I going to do with you. I'll kill you, so I will.' She got the big scissors and came towards me, cut the feathers out of my hair, snapped them and threw them into the fire. 'Let me see you putting anything in your hair again and see what you'll get.'

Clouds of blue smoke began to fill the room. The frying-pan had over-heated and the smell of burning fat was everywhere. 'Now look what you've been the cause of, and your father walking in the door,' she said and slapped me again. The more I cried the more she hit me. I cried louder, hoping my father was coming and would hear me. 'Stop that crying,' she shouted. 'Stop it, d'ye hear me?' Then with a final slap she pushed me away, saying, 'Now you've got something to cry for.' She didn't look a bit like the woman in the picture. Her face was all creased and red and her eyes glared. 'I hate you. I hate you. I wish you were dead,' I said again and again to myself.

'That's him now,' my mother said. 'Stop that crying before he comes in.' I cried louder. My father would be on my side. He loved me the best.

He opened the door and the blue haze escaped on to the landing. 'Jesus Christ Almighty! What's been happening?' he asked her.

'What's been happening is that that one came in with her hair full of tar and feathers. Look at it! Look at the state of it!' She banged the iron pot on the stove trying to dislodge the burnt potatoes. 'It's all your fault,' she continued. 'You have her ruined. She's a self-willed little bitch.'

'Leave her alone. She's only a child. You're always on at her.' I sidled up to him, rubbing my face into his sleeve, forcing out the sobs. His coat smelled lovely. He ran his hand over my hair.

'Sit down and leave your father alone,' my mother said. 'You've caused enough trouble for one day.'

My father had the top potatoes which hadn't scorched. I liked the burnt bits and my mother, as usual, had a portion of dinner on a saucer. After dinner I asked, 'Mammy, can I go out and play, can I?' She had wet a pot of tea and put it on to draw.

'No you can't,' she said. 'Wait and have a cup of tea.' Her anger all gone now. She cut bread and buttered it, talking to my father at the same time. I ate bread and jam and waited for the tea to cool. My father gave her five shillings, and me tuppence, from tips he had made.

'Now can I go?' She was engrossed in what my father was telling her, looking happy, smiling at him.

'Yes, go on and don't go away from the front,' she called after me. I shouted back my agreement and raced down into the sunlit street—the slaps, the tears, tar and feathers all forgotten. John Joe was sitting on the curb by the shore dropping stones into the water. I sat beside him pushing him up a bit so I could throw stones into the grate too.

'Have you seen Hannah?' I asked. He shook his head. Sometimes he answered you, sometimes he didn't. 'Will you go down to her house for me?' He looked sullen and shook his head again. I shoved him and he started to cry. I ran away then shouting, 'John Joe Durkin is no good. Chop him up for firewood.' I wandered down the street looking into shop windows, deciding how to spend my tuppence. I bought a gelatine doll and a balloon on a bamboo stick with red feathers on the mouthpiece. When I came back there was still no sign of Hannah. She must have got into trouble over her runners. If she didn't come soon I'd be stuck with John Joe for the rest of the day. I sat beside him and started to blow up my balloon. I blew hard and the red rubber swelled, the colour changed, paled, and the balloon grew into a rose-pink ball. I took it out of my mouth. The air rushed from it with a squeaking sound. I turned away from him and started to blow again. John Joe clapped his hands as the balloon grew bigger and bigger.

'Me have it. Me have it,' he chanted, pulling at my arm. I jerked it to dislodge him. The balloon shot out of my mouth and sailed into the middle of the road, squeaking as it went. It landed and did a lot of little hops as the air escaped. John Joe, with a squeal of delight, ran after it and straight into the path of a speeding lorry. His body was lifted up and thrown towards the grating. He fell with his head hitting the curb, and his blood, the same colour as the red balloon, ran along the gutter and down into the drain. All the people came running from everywhere. Mrs Durkin came running down the street screaming. I ran away around the corner and into the alley. I climbed the hill and lay down in the grass that grew near the top wall. I kept seeing the blood going down the drain. John Joe was dead and Hannah would tell everyone I had murdered him. My mother would kill me. I still had the doll. One of its legs dangled loosely on the elastic thread. I pulled it off and threw it away.

I lay for a long time. It seemed a long time anyway. It began to get dark. My mother would be looking for me now, calling me. She might think I was dead and be sorry for me. I was very hungry and wanted my tea. I pulled some stalks of grass and chewed them. But I couldn't go home. I could never go home again. I would have to stay here all night. They would put me in prison.

I sat up and looked down the alley. It was nearly dark and the cats were prowling, searching for fish heads. Two started to fight, spitting and snarling at each other. I thought about the dead fish and imagined maggots crawling up the hill to get me. I started to cry. Then I heard the whistle. It was my father, whistling the way he did to call me in. Then I heard him call my name. His footsteps came nearer. I could see him now. He called again.

My sobs became louder, each one hiccuping through my body. He saw me and started up the hill. 'Thank God. Oh, thank God. I've looked everywhere for you.' He wrapped me in his coat and carried me down the hill. I cried all the way home. My mother was at the hall door. She ran to meet us.

'Thanks be to God you're all right.' She rubbed my hair where the feathers had been and hurried us up the stairs. 'Where were you?' she said. 'Where were you at all? I was demented not knowing where you were.' She gave me hot milk and talked all the time about how worried she had been.

'Tell her what happened to John Joe, Mammy,' my brother said. 'Tell her, Mammy.' I closed my eyes pretending I had fallen asleep.

'Poor little John Joe,' she said. 'But wasn't he lucky all the same.'

'What happened to him?'

'He was knocked down after dinner. But someone was praying for him. His head was split open. Fourteen stitches. Thank God he's going to be all right.'

The cup slipped from my fingers onto the hearth, smashing, the milk trickling across the oilcloth.

'Why the bloody hell can't you be more careful? I never knew such a child—always smashing and breaking things.'

It was all right. Everything was all right. Everything as usual. 'I'm tired. I want to go to bed.' I went.

THREE

'Children should have pets,' my father said one evening.

'Oh yes,' replied my mother, who was reading the deaths in the *Herald* and only half listening.

'There's a fella in work has rabbits, white angoras. He said I could have one for nothing.'

'Oh Daddy, Daddy, a bunny rabbit. Can I have it?'

Suddenly my mother was all ears. 'You're bringing no rabbit in here.'

'It's only a small one.'

'I don't care if it's a midget. I've enough to do keeping the room clean without rabbit shite to contend with.'

But my father had a habit of getting his own way and the rabbit came home in a hutch that fitted underneath the sideboard.

'You're out of your mind keeping that thing,' my aunt said the first time she saw Lish. 'Before the week's out the place will smell like the monkey-house in the zoo.'

I sat for hours staring adoringly at the ball of white fluff, longing to touch it. But my mother had eyes in the back of her head and no sooner had my fingers come within inches of the wire netting than she shouted, warning me of missing fingers, blood poisoning and lock-jaw.

The rabbit lasted as long as my father cleaned the cage daily, which wasn't long. While he was in work my mother found a boy with a garden who was delighted to get an angora rabbit for nothing. 'Now let your father open his mouth to me about rabbits when he comes in and I'll give it to him.' All afternoon she primed herself for the anticipated flare-up. She'd tell him one of us could be at death's door, our health destroyed and all on the head of him and his rabbit. Believing always that attack was the best means of defence, the minute he opened the door she fired her shot. But my father was in a hurry to have his tea, he had a union meeting to go to, and wasn't interested in the fate of the rabbit.

I was brokenhearted and to console my grief my mother promised me a kitten. 'In any case', she said, 'a kitten is a better pet. Sure what could you do with a rabbit?' And a kitten came trained by its mother and didn't sit staring at you all day. Not long afterwards the kitten arrived. She was called Woolley and my mother gave her the run of the room except when she grew big enough to jump onto the baby's pram, then Woolley was sent flying.

'It's out of your belly you grow,' was a maxim of my mother's. Others were, 'Good food warms the cockles of your heart, puts firm flesh on your bones, keeps your bowels open and your limbs supple.' Pregnant women, nursing mothers, working men and growing children 'needed stall-feeding'. Women who had the means but curtailed their tables 'wore hunger's muzzle'. Worse were women who sent their children to school on cold potatoes and then gorged their gut on new-laid eggs, toast and bacon—they'd 'never see heaven'.

She spent the majority of her income on food. Sirloin, silverside of corned beef or a shoulder of bacon, sausage and black and white pudding for Saturday tea and Sunday breakfast. Pots of floury potatoes, cabbage, yellow turnips, carrots, porridge, bread in unlimited quantities lavishly buttered, pork-and beef-dripping for fried bread, stewed apple, rhubarb and gooseberries, all were put before us. Tea, cocoa, milk, butter-milk and water there was to drink. Minerals were for special occasions.

Tinned food, tinned milk and margarine were abominations. Tinned food could cause agonizing deaths, margarine was only another name for axle grease and condensed milk had half the country in sanatoriums.

Before her eyes she saw the proof of her belief in good food, healthy children and a husband who could take the stairs two at a time, whistling as he did. Her legs were knotted with varicose veins, but they never caused her a pain or ache and all women who had had children had veins. She was thankful to God for her health. Everything was in his hands. The loss of her first two children was a cross to bear. Her first baby, who was born dead, she hadn't seen. She was in Limbo where unbaptized infants went. Her mother had described the baby to her. A little girl with bracelets of fat on her wrists. My mother called her 'angel' and often talked about her but didn't cry for her. But the other child, a boy who had lived for eleven weeks, she mourned. His eyes, she said, were so blue that the whites of them appeared to be blue as well. She remembered, and repeated, the sound he made when taking her breast. He died after a convulsion and everyone said it was a sin to put such beauty in a coffin. The coffin was too big for him so she packed all of his clothes around him to keep him comfortable, and told me that for months after he died she kept a napkin of his so that she could smell his smell. Fifty years after his death she would still sometimes cry for him and try to imagine the man he might have become.

'A dacent crathur,' was how my mother described the woman who, with her husband and nine children, lived in the other room on the landing. 'A well-reared girl who wouldn't trouble you for the time of day. And he's a little gentleman. A good father who's out in the spills of rain riding that oul' messenger bike delivering provisions. Isn't it a crying shame when a man can only get a boy's work?'

She and her neighbour had amicable arrangements about cleaning the stairs and lavatory and sharing the line. However, my mother's amicability did not extend to sharing the prime spot outside the salt shop where she liked to air the baby, and every morning there was a race to get our baby down first. My mother almost always won. After bumping the pram down the stairs she returned for the baby and made the second journey up the stairs singing at the top of her voice, having left the baby contentedly playing with a stiff blue sugar bag, rattling the few remaining grains, and as the morning went on, reefing the bag to bits.

When the baby was brought back to the room scraps of blue paper littered the pram. No one ever thought of piecing them together and if they had, would have assumed that the missing pieces had blown away in the wind. Until the baby's head-cold lingered and my mother noticed a peculiar smell coming from her nose. Investigating, she discovered that one of the child's nostrils was jammed solid with slimy blue paper.

'Sacred Heart of Jesus if she inhaled that she's done for. What'll I do?' she asked and she answered herself, 'Get her up to the Eye and Ear.'

'I'll ask Mrs Doyle to keep and eye on him,' she said nodding in my brother's direction, 'and leave a note for your father. Wouldn't you know it, the very night I could do with him being here he's late home. You can come with me. Hold the child while I take the pram down.' And once more she bumped the pram down the flights of stairs.

It was Saturday evening. The shops would be open late. She would buy me a cake and a glass of milk from the dairy, maybe something else. I was delighted to be going with her. We left my brother with the neighbour and set off. 'We'll go the canal way, it's a bit longer but a nicer walk.' There were boys swimming in the canal and my mother forecast a watery grave for every one of them and wondered what sort of parents they had, letting them swim in the weed-clogged dirty water.

'It's a pity, all the same, that your daddy isn't with us,' she said when we had passed the boys. 'I'd have enjoyed the ramble with him. We used to walk along here when I was going with him.' She pointed out a little house on the far side of the canal water and said it was where she lived when she first married. 'The Lord have mercy on my mother, she got it for me. A little dog box and walking alive with rats. I killed one of them once. A big fella the size of a cat.'

I wasn't expected to make any comment so only half listened to what she was saying and watched the water pouring into the lock while we waited to cross the road. Then turned into a tree-lined road where every house had a garden full of flowers and some of the doors wore sunshades of brightly striped canvas. There were no children playing in the street, everywhere was quiet and peaceful.

We had to wait a long time before a doctor saw us. 'A bit of a thick,' was how my mother described him when he left the cubicle for a moment. He took a long time to free the baby's nostril; the slimy paper disintegrating under the tweezers. The baby screamed and my mother talked, telling me I should have kept an eye on her. 'But Mammy,' I protested, 'I wasn't with her.'

'Don't back answer me.' She slapped me across the arm and looked in the doctor's direction for a word of approval. The doctor, engrossed in removing the last slithery morsel, said nothing.

She'd have liked a comment that the baby was a fine child,

pretty, well-looked after, that she was right to chastise me for answering back. However, had the word been critical she would have told him that if it wasn't for the likes of her and babies pushing things up their noses there'd be no call for the likes of him. For she always thought of the right thing to say at the right time. 'A student, that's all that fella was, outta the College of Surgeons,' she said after putting a shilling in the almoner's box.

We went home a different way. Through a busy street full of shops. Clothes shops and shoe shops. Provision shops with lovely smells coming out of the doors, smells of cheese and bacon, smells that made you hungry. Outside the butcher's there were brine barrels full of pickling tongues, corned beef and pigs' legs. I looked in through the doors at the sawdust-covered floors, dirty now at the end of the day, and at the men with their blood-stained overalls. Shoes hung in hanks like onions, and outside one shop my mother fancied a pair of pale blue ones for the baby. They were stiff and shiny and fastened with a button on the ankle. The assistant undid the shoes from the hank and pushed them on the baby's feet. My mother handed over one and six. 'Leave the shoes on her,' she said. 'She looks a little dote in them.'

I got my cake, a jam-soaked doughnut and a glass of milk. My mother bought a quarter of cow-heel for the supper. The baby fell asleep. When we got home the woman on the landing said my father had been and gone out again. 'To a union meeting, he said. I told him I'd keep the child here till you came back. Is the baby all right?'

'Grand thanks, and thanks very much.' My brother was asleep. The woman carried him into the room and my mother laid him in the bed, only taking off his shoes. Her lips were screwed up into a tight purse. The baby had wet herself, soaking the new shoes. The pale blue shiny stuff peeled away from the canvas lining. She took them off the child and threw them into the fire, throwing the quarter of cow-heel after them. The dying flames revived round the grease from the meat, burning fiercely for a moment, then subsided.

'You get ready for bed while I make you a sup of cocoa,' she said, moving about the room, her face clouded with anger.

There were lace hangings on the windows. My mother's pride and joy. One morning after the baby had been put down for her airing and my aunt had taken my brother out for the day,

I looked around the room for something to do. The kitten ran under the bed when I went to pick it up. My colouring book was all crayoned in. 'Can I go down to play, Mammy?' I asked.

'No you can't, you've got a cold. I'm going down to the yard for water and don't pull the place about.'

I went to look out through the window. A curtain hung round my head. It felt like the veils girls wore for their Holy Communion and to walk in the May procession. I arranged it closer round me. Then I began to twirl, slowly at first, then faster and faster I spun, enjoying the slightly painful sensation as the hanging tightened its hold on my hair. The dust from the curtain tickled my nose. The room rotated, familiar objects blurred, took on strange and wonderful shapes. The bamboo curtain-pole strained under my weight. I kept spinning until my hair became so entangled in the lace that the aching sweetness in my scalp changed to a smarting soreness that made me begin to untwirl. Gradually the room came back into focus. The double bed ceased to heave and the red linoleum lay still on the floor. The table, sideboard and chairs rested in their proper places. And the picture of the woman in the long white dress lay flat once more on the wall. Deliciously dizzy I staggered away from the window and walked around the room, hands outstretched to steady myself.

A sound of footsteps and the clanking of metal warned me my mother was coming. Climbing the stairs, she stopped now and then to rest the buckets, letting the handles strike the sides of the pail. I ran quickly to the window to tidy the folds of the curtains and saw the long tear in the lace. 'Please God, don't let her see it. I'll be killed, please God don't let her notice,' I prayed. I could smell the clothes boiling on the stove—maybe if they were boiling over? I wasn't supposed to touch the gas, but I did, going to the cooker and highering the flame. Grey soap-bubbles crept up the side of the tin-pot, hovered on its side for a second, burst, and water cascaded down onto the jet of gas. I busied myself pretending to colour a picture that was already coloured, at the same time looking up from under my eyes to see if the torn curtain would be noticed.

'You bloody little bitch. You've been at the curtains. I can't leave you for five minutes but you're pulling the place about. Look at it. It's in ribbons. You little sleeveen, sitting there with your painting book after destroying my hangings.' To say nothing was usually the safest thing, so I said nothing. 'I've told you time and time again not to touch near them. Do you hear what I'm telling you?' Still I said nothing but looked at my mother. 'I'll take that look of derision off your face,' she said and came to where I sat and slapped me across the face. It was a stinging slap that made me cry. 'What are you crying for,' she shouted. 'I'll kill you so I will if you don't stop that whingeing. Do you hear me? Stop that crying for nothing. Stop it. One of these days you'll bring the pole down on top of you.' She slapped me again. 'Now you've got something to cry for,' she said. She always said that after the second slap. It never hurt as much as the first one and I knew that in a minute she'd stop giving out and start doing something else. But not yet, for her face was still red and angry-looking and I thought again how she didn't look at all like the woman in the picture. I was sobbing still, having to force it a bit now. She knew, as she always did, and said, 'And you can stop that play-acting. Anyone would think I'd murdered you.'

She noticed the smell of escaping gas, turned it off, and still giving out about the torn curtains and how I could have been killed stone dead if the pole had fallen on my head, began preparations to do the washing. Moving two chairs close to each other she put a tin bath across them, lifted the boiling pot from the stove and tipped in the clothes, added cold water from a bucket and began to rub and scrub the clothes on the washboard. As if soothed by the warm water, gradually the anger and harassed expression left her face and she began to sing in a high sweet voice. She looked lovely. I loved her when she sang and was sorry for tearing the curtain. And sorry for her poor hands that after the washing would be sore from the soda, and the cracks in them would open again.

I moved quietly near the window, not near enough to touch the curtains and make her shout again, but near enough to play with the dusty sunbeams, fingering them, trying to hold them. I seemed to be there for a long time when the singing stopped and I looked around. My mother was lifting a towel from the bath, wringing it, grimacing, winding the wrung-out part around her arm where it lay like a damp snake. Then looking at the clock she exclaimed, 'Look at the time. Your father'll be in in a minute and I've nothing for his tea. You'll have to go down to Allen's and get a quarter of tinned beef and a Spanish onion.'

23

She dried her hands. 'Stop foostering there by the window and come on.' She counted out the money and made me repeat what I was going for. And as I went out the door called after me, 'And don't lose the money and don't pick the meat'. I ran down the stairs, stopping in the hall to work my finger round the hole in the red-raddled wall. Pieces of black horsehair bonded the mortar. I pulled out a piece making the hole huge then licked my fingers. I liked the taste of plaster. I got the meat and onion and picked a morsel of the tinned beef near the edge where it mightn't be noticed and ate it.

When I came back the washing was folded in a neat pile, the bath put away and the table laid for tea. My mother was tidying the room, then tidying herself, taking off the pinnie she had worn to do the washing, putting on a clean one, looking at herself in the mirror, smoothing the coils of dark brown hair she wore pinned over her ears. Talking out loud to herself, 'I hope he's in good humour. I hope he hasn't anything on for the night.'

I listened for my father's whistling. My wonderful father would be coming soon. 'There he is, there he is. Can I go out and meet him? Can I Mammy?' I had the door open and was gone without waiting for an answer, running down the stairs, jumping the last steps into his waiting arms, winding mine around his neck and laying my cheek next to his, breathing in his gorgeous smell, a mixture of horses and tobacco and his own body scent. I rubbed my face against his, it was prickly. 'What did you bring me Daddy? What did you bring me,' I asked, nuzzling him.

'That's a nice way to greet me. No kiss, nothing only what did I bring you.'

'I love you. I love you the best in the whole world.' I kissed his face and hugged him tighter. Every night we followed the same ritual. The jump into his outstretched arms, the questions, his pretended scolding, the kiss and my declaration of love. Then he would carry me up the stairs. But tonight, for the first time ever, he said when we reached the first landing, 'I'll have to put you down. I'm bunched. You're getting too heavy for me.'

'Ah no,' I protested and reluctantly allowed myself to be put down. 'I'll hold your hand,' I said, and hand in hand we climbed the remaining stairs and as we went into the room I once more asked, 'What did you bring me?'

'You have her ruined,' my mother said.

'She's only a child,' my father said.

'A spoiled child that knows how to wind you around her finger.'

My father didn't answer that remark. Reaching into his pocket he told me to shut my eyes, put out my hand and see what God had sent me. I screwed my eyes up tight and stretched out my hands. Immediately I felt something touch them. I opened my eyes and saw scraps of stiff white satin lace.

'You can make clothes for your doll.'

'They're lovely, lovely and silky,' I said, running my thumbs across the material. Every night he brought me a present. Sometimes pencils or a bag of beads to thread into a necklace. A story-book, bars of chocolate, small wooden blocks of polished oak, with which my brother and I built walls and houses without windows. The building bricks and scraps of material for dolly clothes were from the coffin-shop, but they were only wood and material, they didn't frighten me, not like real coffins. I didn't like them. People were always being put into them and couldn't move or talk. My mother was always taking me to see people in coffins. A little girl the size of me with her stomach all swollen and a woman who used to give me a penny when she passed me sitting on the step. She had a swollen stomach too. And then one day I saw her in a coffin and there was a baby tucked in by her feet.

'Put those things away and sit over for your tea,' my mother said. I came to the table where my mother was cutting bread. My father pushed the meat and onion about his plate.

'What's the matter with it? I thought you liked tinned beef?'

'I'm not hungry. I've that pain in my chest again,' my father said.

Her lips tightened as she sawed through the loaf. 'So would I if I stayed out half the night. Wind, that's all it is.'

'Have you any Andrews?'

'It's tall orders you have. Where would I get Andrews?'

'A bit of bread soda then?'

My mother mixed the bread soda and water. 'Ugh,' my father said and made a face.

'Will I cook something else, a rasher and egg?' my mother asked, taking the cup from him. He smiled at her and said no that he felt better. 'Sit over to the fire and I'll wet fresh tea.

Maybe a bit of toast, could you eat that?' She fussed over him, telling him to rest, to go to bed early.

'I can't tonight. There's a removal but I'll be home by eight.'

Later my aunt brought the baby and my brother home. They were palmed out, she said, from all the fresh air and would be asleep in no time. When they were, I sat on her lap and listened while my mother talked about my father. 'He wasn't well. He keeps getting a pain in his chest.'

'It's far from his arse—he won't sit on it,' my aunt said. 'Where is he now?'

'On a removal and you needn't look like that, it's genuine enough.'

'Watch him, all the same.'

I wondered why he should be watched but didn't ask.

'Whether he's in or out is none of your business,' my mother said in a tone of annoyance.

'You make it my business by giving me all your information,' my aunt retorted.

'Well I won't in future.'

'Suit yourself and drop the talk. This one's all ears,' my aunt replied and squeezed me affectionately. 'When are you coming down to see me again?' she asked.

'Maybe tomorrow or sometime. Have you still got Prince?'

'I have and you can look at him.'

'And will you tell me all about him?'

'Every bit about him.'

'It's time you got ready for bed,' my mother said.

'Do I have to?'

'You do this minute.'

I tried to stay awake. If I could my father would be home and would take me up if I let on to have a bad dream. And then I'd be up late. The next thing I knew it was morning and my father was getting ready for work. I lay and watched him shaving, putting up the strop on a hook, running his gleaming razor up and down the leather, testing it with his thumb, then covering his face with lather until you could only see his eyes, nose and lips. He looked like a snowman we once built in the yard.

FOUR

It was cold enough for snow, my father said when November came. Then the cold went and the rain came. Lashing down every day, hopping like darts on the path, running down the window-panes so that it was hard to see out. I had another cold and my mother rubbed my chest with camphorated oil, first warming it by placing the bottle near the hob. The rubbing tickled and I laughed and squirmed but cried when I had to drink the hip-o'-wine and squills which was supposed to cure my cough.

Unless you were seriously ill the doctoring was done at home. Sometimes the chemist's advice was asked, but usually the cures were ones with which my mother was familiar. Medicines and ointments her own mother used. Bread poultices for festerings, healing and drawing ointment for sores, vaseline for almost everything, boracic powder for stuping wounds and bathing sore eyes. Red flannel for sore throats, blessed at a yearly ceremony held in honour of St Blaise who had choked on a fish bone. Hip-o'-wine and squills for children's coughs and Famel Syrup for adults.

Because of the weather and my cold I wasn't allowed to go with my father to do the stabling. I missed the trip for the first week but staying at home with my mother on Sunday mornings had its compensations. Having balls of pastry to make jam tarts with, listening to her singing while she prepared the vegetables. Cutting the white juicy stalks from the cabbage and telling me to eat them—they were good for me. Hearing stories of the olden days when she was young.

The smell of roasting meat filled the room, the table was laid and the custard and jelly set on the window-sill. My father came back and brought sweets and chocolates. My mother and he talked about what he had seen when he was out, laughing and joking. And then my father said it would soon be Christmas and he'd give my mother extra money to take us to see Daddy Christmas.

The little shops put up green and red balls and stuck pieces of cotton wool all over their windows, and sold wooden lambs and horses on wheeled wooden platforms with scraps of fur stuck on for tails and manes. My mother counted up how much she had paid into her Ham Club. Not as much as she thought and she resolved that next year she would do better. Start the payments earlier, throw a few shillings into the Ham Club every week when she bought her provisions. My father told her not to worry—he would see her all right for Christmas—she could have all his tips. 'That'll be grand,' she said and continued talking about Christmas. How lovely it would be to have a Christmas tree. No one she knew had ever had one. And she wondered what Christmas box the grocer would give her. God knew she spent enough with him. She should get a cake. Not that she liked pink-iced cakes. But every week she left him a handful and last year all he gave her was a calendar. A calendar that wouldn't have cost tuppence in Woolworths. Not even a Christmas candle. Well he'd get an awful suck-in if he tried that on this year. Not another ha'penny of her money would he ever handle again.

Three days before Christmas my father came in at dinnertime carrying a Christmas tree. 'Oh,' my mother said, 'that's beautiful. Where did you get that? Smell it, it's like the pine forest. Where did you get it?'

'From a fella in Mount Jerome.'

'Honest to God.'

'Honest to God.'

'I can't believe it—a real Christmas tree! Wait'll you see the way I'll decorate it. Only listen, don't mention to anyone that it came from the cemetery. It wouldn't sound right.'

'Why,' asked my father.

'Because you know very well what they'd say. "Them and their Christmas tree. They're welcome to it. Maybe pulled out of a grave. You wouldn't have an hour's luck with a tree like that."'

My father laughed and said she was mad but agreed to go along with her deception. The tree was decked in yards of shimmering tinsel and hung with coloured glass balls and I stood before it spellbound, thinking that tinsel was what fairies must wear when they danced in the moonlight. The tree was the most beautiful, enchanting thing I had ever seen and I never wanted to stop looking at it.

'What's Daddy Christmas bringing you?' I was asked by my aunt and relations.

'A big white Christmas stocking, isn't he Mammy?'

'Daddy Christmas has more sense. Bloody rubbish them things is. Catchpenny things, a lot of white net stuffed with rubbish. If you're a good girl maybe he'll bring you a doll.' I didn't want a doll. Their hair got tangled and they lost their shoes. I wanted a Christmas stocking and everyday I looked at them in the shop and hoped I would get one instead of a doll. But on Christmas morning there was no stocking on the bed, only two cardboard boxes. 'The biggest one is yours,' my mother said. 'Open it and see what he brought.' Maybe the stocking was inside the box, I thought, as I tore off the paper and opened the box. But it was a doll. A baby doll in pink knitted clothes, wearing a bonnet and bootees like a real baby's. 'Take it out,' my mother said, 'only be careful—its head is made of china.'

'It hasn't got any eyes,' I said.

'It has. Lift it up. It's a sleeping doll.'

As carefully as I would have handled a baby, I picked up the doll and her eyes opened, beautiful blue, blue eyes.

'Now isn't that better than an oul' stocking?' my mother asked, smiling at me.

It was, and it wasn't, though I said 'yes'. My brother had a painted wooden cart that could be pushed and pulled along, and the baby some soft toys. As well as opening and closing her eyes the doll, when you turned her over, said 'Mama'. I spent most of the morning turning her over as I sat in front of the tree admiring it and inhaling the smell of greenness and pine.

It was the custom for the neighbours to call before dinner and sample the Christmas pudding and if, unlike my mother, they took a drink, have a small glass of port. Everyone extolled the virtues of my mother's pudding. She returned their visits and afterwards regaled us with descriptions of the cakes and puddings she had tasted, likening most of them to dogshite.

In the afternoon the relations came, bringing Christmas presents. Books and toys, sweets and games, and one who worked in a stationer's, pencils, rubbers and coloured markers. Then my aunt arrived with a big brown paper parcel and a tin drum and drumstick for my brother. 'Open it,' she said, handing me the packet. I reefed off the paper, guessing, hoping, so excited that she had to help me undo the final wrapping. And there was the longest, fattest, white-net, red-trimmed Christmas stocking I had ever seen. The lockstitch which fastened the top was undone and I plunged my hand into a never-ending lucky dip. Out came a moneybox, a set of snakes and ladders, a brightly painted whistle, a wooden top, a box of chalks, a bag of marbles, a cardboard sweetshop complete with miniature sweet jars and a little pair of scales, and still there were piles of things stuffed all the way down to the toe. I was overwhelmed with the amount and variety and didn't know what to play first. My brother marched round the room banging his drum and when my aunt had gone, my mother took it from him. To my father she said, 'I'm sure that wan did that to annoy me. Mad jealous of the Christmas tree. Why else would she bring a drum to send me out of my mind, and buy a Christmas stocking after I refused to get one.'

I listened from the bed where the baby doll, divested of her woollen layette, slept beside me, her head, with its smooth-moulded hair that would never tangle, on my pillow. On the bedpost hung my stocking.

'I wouldn't say that,' my father said.

'That's you all over, taking anyone's part but mine.'

Her voice sounded tired and cross. They might have a row and spoil the day. I wanted to go to sleep before they did. Before they went to bed, put out the light and everything went away in the dark.

Sundays and Christmas Day were special days but Monday always came and with it my mother's bad humour. Her money was all spent, the rent-man was calling and the week to be got through. Clothes— my father's best suit, overcoat and my camel coloured coat with brown silk arrows highlighting the pleats— were taken from the wardrobe, scrutinized for soiling, creases, missing buttons or any wear and tear; repaired, brushed, sponged and pressed, put into a large brown paper bag and taken to the pawn. Pawning was no disgrace, I'd heard my mother say several times. What you pledged was your own. The highest in the land had done it; kings and gentlemen pawned their plate and jewels. Yet when I was old enough to accompany her I realized the shame and embarrassment she suffered going into pawn. Using a cubicle in which to conduct her transactions and pledging in her maiden name—a useless ploy as the assistant's voice was loud and carried into the public section packed with our neighbours who knew my mother better by her single name.

'Ten shillings on the suit, Tom.'

'Seven and six,' Tom replied.

'Ah Tom, are you codding me, it's brand new. Not a brack on it. Make it nine bob.'

'Eight shillings,' Tom's voice intoned.

'May God forgive you; eight and six.'

'Eight shillings.' Tom's voice had a finality about it. Already he was writing out the ticket.

'You're a terrible man,' my mother replied, secretly relieved she hadn't been cut more.

On Friday night or Saturday morning the clothes were released for the weekend. The levy had already been charged on the ticket at the time of pawning. The clothes smelled of the pawn, a mixture of camphor and of being stored with so many other used garments. So that even after the first pawning they never felt new anymore. Something was gone from them and even in warm weather they had a damp cold feeling about them.

From time to time my mother would console herself that one day, once she was on the pig's back, she would never again have to set foot in a pawn office. And that in any case she still hadn't been reduced to pawning the bedclothes, ornaments nor her wedding ring. Nor stripping my father of his working clothes when he came in at the weekend like the woman she knew, the wife of a tradesman in constant work. An eejit of a man who stood in his drawers and vest while his wife ran with his overalls and pawned them so she could release his suit for mass. And on Monday morning the same man waited patiently in his underwear for his wife to pledge the good suit and get out his working clothes. And all because the woman was too fond of the bookie's office.

'All the same, isn't your fella a picture. I do stand to look after him.'

'Indeed he's not,' my mother preened as she denied my father's good looks to the woman we had met at the corner of the street.

'Go away outta that. He is so. But all the same I wouldn't

like my husband to be that handsome—not with the young wans that's in it nowadays.'

My mother made an excuse that she was in a hurry, would have to go. Holding my hand so tightly that it hurt, she rushed me down the street to her sister's, where the minute we were in the door she said, 'I'm dropping, give me a glass of water.'

'What ails you—you're not in the way again?' my aunt said as she brought the water and a glass of minerals for me.

'No I am not. I met that Lily McGennis at Leonard's Corner and she as much as told me the other fella's carrying on.'

'Well you've had your suspicions.'

'That's a different thing altogether to someone giving you the bang of it up into the face.'

'Your suspicions were once well founded. Didn't you meet him once with a girl hanging out of his arm and you not six months married?'

'That was years ago. I've had no bother since—well as far as I know.'

'Can I look at Prince?' I asked.

'Of course you can love. Go on with what you were telling me about, Aggie.'

With my back to the two of them while I looked at the stuffed dog in its glass case, I could hear what they were saying.

'You know the begrudger she is. Wouldn't say you looked well if you were decked in diamonds. And all of a sudden she's full of praise for him. I should have been on my guard.'

'Which, of course you weren't, not once she started praising him. That's you all over—very romantic.'

'Can I open the case and touch Prince?'

'Do love.'

'Don't be so cutting—it's nothing to do with being romantic—he is the handsomest man in the street.' I could hear the change in my mother's voice. In a minute she'd get her rag out.*

'He is that right enough,' my aunt said. 'The kettle's boiling. Tell me what else that wan said while I wet the tea.'

'That I'd want to watch him with the young wans. She was alluding to something—I'm no fool. Giving me a rub. I should

---

* Lose her temper.

32

have challenged her but I was choked and couldn't get away from her fast enough.'

'Did you say nothing?'

'I told you—I was choked.'

'You must have been—I've never known you at a loss for a word. Where would he meet young wans?'

I stroked the dog's stiff fur. His eyes didn't move. 'How old are young wans, Mammy?' I asked, remembering the girl who had given me the chocolate. My mother didn't answer me but continued talking to her sister.

'He goes nowhere except to union meetings. You wouldn't meet them there nor in the job. I wish to God I hadn't bumped into that wan. My mind won't rest easy now.'

'Drink the tea before it gets cold. Lily's a blather as well as a begrudger. She mightn't have meant anything. And anyway, it's no use meeting trouble half way. But in the meantime keep your eyes open. Search his pockets—you'd never know what you'd find.'

'If there's any truth in it I'd leave him. I'd never lay a-side on a bed with him again.'

'Like you did when you found him out in the beginning. Get sense will you. Then, you didn't have chick nor child. You could have gone back to work. Where would you go now with three children? Who'd keep you? Poison him. Trip him up on the stairs or do like the woman did years ago in Newmarket—a job with a pair of shears.'

My mother spluttered laughing. 'God forgive you—you're a terrible woman,' she said and I knew she wasn't angry at the moment.

'Tell me about Prince,' I said, sidling up to my aunt who put her arms around me.

'Come over here and sit on my lap,' my mother said, holding out her arms.

'I don't want to.' I leant closer to my aunt.

'Do what you're told, come over here.'

'Leave the child alone.' My aunt, like my father, always took my side.

'Tell me about Prince,' I said and my mother gave me a look that promised trouble later.

'Prince was the loveliest dog in the world. The bravest and the fiercest dog you could find anywhere. And talk about clever!

He could beg and give you the paw and before I'd put my coat on he'd know I was going out. I had him for years. He was very old and when he got sick and died I couldn't bear to part with him so a man on the quays stuffed him and now I've got him for ever and ever.'

'Did you have him when he was a pup?'

'From the time he was that size, not much bigger than my hand. And a terrible handful he was. Do you know he ate dozens of pairs of shoes. Chawed the backs out of them and left me in my bare feet. And a robber, too. You couldn'y leave a bit of meat out of the press or he'd be off with it. And another day he got the wool I was knitting with and tangled it so much—like a spider's web it was the way he had dragged it round the legs of the chairs.'

I was laughing so much I nearly cried. My mother said I was making too much noise. And my aunt said I wasn't and not to be venting her spleen on a child. Then my mother jumped up and said we were going home immediately and told her sister never to interfere again when she was chastizing her own child. Outside she told me that if I didn't stop crying and making a show of her she would give me something to cry for. Knowing she would never hit me in the street, I bawled. She began to talk. About Prince. 'Her and her dog. A whole lot of lies that is. She never owned a dog in her life. She bought him stuffed and all. Prince how are you. He was that long in the Iveagh Market it's a wonder they didn't crown him King never mind Prince.' Then it wasn't true! All my aunt had told me was lies. No Prince. No pup as big as her hand. I walked slowly. My mother told me to stop dragging my feet. It began to rain. I put out my tongue to catch the drops. Maybe there was no Father Christmas either, nor fairies. 'Will you do what you're told or do I have to talk to you again? Stop dragging your feet and hurry up and mind that puddle. I'm telling you, the sooner you go to school, the better.'

* * *

'Be a good girl, do what you're told and put your hand up if you want to go to the lavatory,' my mother said as she got me ready for my first morning at school. 'I went there and your granny before me,' she said as she woolled at the back of my hair

34

where it fuzzed after sleeping on it. 'Turn round and let me have a look at you. You'll do,' she said giving a last touch to my fringe. With my hand in hers we went through the school gate. What seemed like hundreds and hundreds of children ran and screamed in a vast sea of concrete. 'That's the playground and that's the shed where you shelter if it's raining.' On up the slope we went, my mother chatting to other women taking their children to school for the first time. 'It's only like yesterday my mother was taking me by the hand to the babies. All the years!' one woman said.

'It hasn't changed much,' my mother said. And the woman replied, 'I hope the nuns have—bloody oul' garrons some of them were.'

'Some of them were,' my mother agreed. 'Do you remember the day the man from Meath Street came to lambast one of them with his brushes—he was a sweep. Straight into the classroom he came full of soot and made a run at her. "You bloody oul' bitch to lay hands on my daughter." We were delighted. But then the Reverand Mother came and threatened him with the police.'

I was taking in every word, imagining the sweep with his black face and hands charging the nun. And then we were there and a nun was talking to my mother and then writing my name in a book. And telling me that school was grand and to wait for a minute and someone would show me to the babies. My mother kissed me and gave me a list of instructions the same as she had when she was getting me ready that morning. I wasn't sad or frightened. I liked the room we were in with coloured holy pictures and vases of flowers and a big fire blazing behind the fireguard. There were smells of chalk and milk in the babies and the smell of knickers that hadn't been washed. We sat on a bench in a row with long tables in front of us. We were told not to talk and to listen. We said our prayers—first in English, then repeating them after the nun in Irish. A girl in front of me started to cry and the nun brought her to the front of the class and petted her and sat her by the fire and after a while she stopped crying but stayed by the fire. We sang songs and clapped hands. School, I thought, was lovely—until I wanted to go to the lavatory and, remembering my mother's instructions, put up my hand. The nun told me where to go. I had no trouble finding the lavatory, but once there, wished I had never come.

There was a fierce old woman with her face all lines wearing a straw Breton hat, who asked in an angry voice what I wanted, and without waiting for an answer told me to hurry up, to pull the chain and not throw anything down the pan. All the time she talked she pushed a mop through milky puddles of Jeyes Fluid. I felt sick from the smell and always remember the lavatories as somewhere awash with Jeyes Fluid where a cranky-faced woman mopped at the puddles with a grey, dirty, long-haired mop.

We sang more songs and learned how to count and in what seemed like no time the bell was ringing and it was time to go home to dinner. My mother met me and asked if I had been a good girl and didn't listen when I told her about the old woman, for she was rushing home. She was always rushing and seldom had time or the mind to listen so that gradually I stopped telling her anything unless it was very startling.

After a week I was able to go down the lane on my own and in a little while knew the names of everyone in my class and the nun knew the name of every child.

FIVE

'And the priest said that people from all over the world will be coming to Dublin. It's a great honour to have the Eucharistic Congress here.'

'That's twice you've told me. What's it all in aid of?' my father asked.

'If you'd have been in mass yesterday you'd have heard the priest explaining. He said that people are too wrapped-up in the ways of the world. Forgetting what they are on earth for. The Eucharistic Congress is to make us realize we're only here to save our souls.'

'Oh yes!' my father said.

'And,' my mother continued, 'after reading out the Bishop's letter, the priest asked everyone to make a special effort to show their devotion to the Blessed Sacrament. To decorate our homes and the streets. You know like, to show outward signs as well. There'll be things on sale in the repository, special things for it.'

'I'm bloody sure there will. When did you ever know the priests miss a chance to make money?'

My mother was ironing a shirt. She spat on the face of the iron to judge the heat before answering my father. 'That's the Protestant drop coming out in you.'

'I'm only repeating what you're always saying. That you wouldn't like to be depending on the priest's charity. That you have to pay your admission fee into mass and are charged a different rate for where you want to sit.'

'That's nothing to do with the Eucharistic Congress. It's ...' But my father wouldn't let her finish.

'And complaining about the men outside pushing collection boxes up into your face.'

'That's got nothing to do with religion. Nothing to do with

37

the Blessed Sacrament,' my mother said, going to the stove to reheat the iron. 'And in any case, won't the decorations be a pleasure? That sort of thing is good for people. Where are you off to tonight?'

'A union meeting,' my father replied before beginning to shave for the second time that day. 'Will you be long with the shirt?'

My mother brought back the iron and banged it on the cuff of the shirt, pressing with unnecessary force. I looked from her angry face to my father's lovely one, from which, with long smooth strokes he removed the barely visible stubble, then raised his nose between finger and thumb to shave his upper lip.

'They'll be making you a big bug in the union with all the meetings you're going to,' my mother said, using the voice which she did before having a row. If they had a row she wouldn't read me a story. It was all her fault. Why couldn't she be like him, never cranky, never starting rows.

'Did you hear what I said?' she asked as she put the shirt over the back of the chair.

'Mmm,' he said as he finished his upper lip.

'Well answer me then. You're going out every other night in the week.'

He was cleaning his razor, folding it, putting it beside its twin in the leather case. 'I have to go, honestly. I'm sorry. It's an important one.' He went and stood by her, looking down at her, smiling. 'Look, I won't even stop for a drink.' He touched her cheek. My mother's cross face disappeared and she smiled at him, and I knew they had forgotten I was in the room.

'I'll tell you what—I'll help you to get the decorations—you can have all my tips. You'll have the best display in the street.'

All the funerals in the coming weeks must have been those of well-off people for my father brought home few tips. And my mother would talk aloud when she and I were alone, wondering where the money was coming from for the decorations she had set her heart on. 'Two pounds would do it. Pay for the bark, the flowers and a few bob to a fella who'd knock-up the window-box, and I'd have oceans left for the velvet and braid to make the banner.'

She considered a Jewman for a loan. But that would mean him calling every week and if my father found out there would be murder. She could miss the rent but unless she missed it for eight weeks and risked eviction that was no use. 'I'll have to ask St Jude, though God knows she's not in any hurry getting me a Corporation house.'

* * *

The time for the Eucharistic Congress was drawing near and St Jude still hadn't answered my mother's prayer for a windfall. Then one day after I came home from school there was a knock on the door and I heard an unfamiliar voice calling, 'Aggie, Aggie Fox are you in?'

My mother hurried to open the door and exclaimed, 'God Almighty! I don't believe it. After all these years. Molly Dignam! Where were you this long time? Come in, come in.' She was so pleased and excited she kept repeating herself while the woman came in, took off her coat and sat down.

'I can't get over it! I was only thinking about you the other night. Wait now till I put the kettle on. I'm delighted to see you.'

Eventually I was introduced, my brother told off for not saying hello and the baby admired by the visitor. Then we were told to either sit up on the bed or look out through the window and keep quiet.

'Aggie,' the woman said, 'you haven't changed a bit and you've kept your lovely figure.'

My mother laughed and ran her hands down her slim hips and across her flat stomach and said, 'Indeed I haven't. Three children and two misses I've had. But sure you look lovely yourself.'

Molly was fat. Her feet were tiny and her hands dimpled. When she laughed her breasts shook. She said I was lovely and the image of my mother, but wasn't sure who my brother or the baby looked like. 'The spittin' image of their father. Of course, I forget—you never met him,' my mother said as she wet the tea. She talked about my father, telling Molly he was English, where he worked, how good he was. Then lamenting that she and Molly hadn't seen each other for years.

'But sure with you living over the northside you might as well be in Timbuctoo. So tell me, what brings you this way? And how is Kevin? If I'd known you were coming I'd have got a cake or a few biscuits. But anyway, have a bit of turnover, and the

39

jam is lovely. None of your mixed fruit that does be yellow turnips dyed. Now tell me all about yourself.'

Molly drank some of the tea and ate some of the bread, then said, 'It's like a dream seeing you again. Didn't we have grand times, all the same? Remember the hooleys and dances?'

'Indeed I do,' my mother said, pushing the plate of buttered turnover towards Molly and urging her to eat. 'Many's the time I think about them. Hold on a minute till I fix the table—I don't want it wobbling and spilling the tea in your lap.' She bent and adjusted the wedge of cardboard, gave cuts of bread to me and my brother, sat down and asked Molly for all her news. They talked and laughed and reminisced until, at last, their excitement wore itself out and my mother asked again what had brought Molly over the southside.

'I've been up to the hospice,' Molly brushed the crumbs from her lap and reached for another slice of bread. 'Kevin's on his last.'

'Oh Jesus, Molly, that's terrible! I'm awful sorry.' My mother put down her cup. 'What ails him?'

'Consumption, like his oul' cow of a mother before him. Don't waste your sympathy on him. The sooner he goes the better.'

My mother choked on the piece of bread she was eating and her face looked the way it did when my aunt said something at which she didn't know whether to laugh or be outraged. After a minute and a few coughs she excused herself saying, 'I have a terrible small swally. All the same, I am sorry—poor Kevin on his last.'

'We'll all be on our last sometime. Because he is won't make me say one thing and think another. He gave me a terrible life. And when he's stretched stiff up and down from his navel I'll dance for joy. He was a louser, a dirty louser. Black and blue he bet me. And every time we had a row threw up at me that he never knew if my first child was his. An animal, that's what he was. Every ten months he had me in the way and every child born dead. An animal would have more respect for its mate. But not him, oh no. The nurse was no sooner out of the room and he'd want me. And on top of everything else he was a lazy bastard. It wasn't through hard work he got consumption.'

'May God comfort you, you've had a terrible life,' my mother said.

40

'Don't be talking. I could write a book on my life. A lazy bastard, lying on his arse morning, noon, and night when he wasn't in his mother's being stall-fed or in the public house drinking the money she gave him knowing that me and the child was in want.'

Sitting on the bed I listened not understanding most of what was being said. Remembering it now from the numerous times I heard the story of Molly's life related as I grew up.

After my mother had shown that her sympathy was all with Molly they talked of other things. Of their youth, of people they hadn't seen for years. Recalling their time in the bakehouse, Molly asking, 'Do you remember the gas there was the day I fecked the icing sugar?'

My mother couldn't remember. 'Ah God, you do,' Molly said. 'I took it for your father. He was dying. During the war. Remember. You couldn't get a grain of sugar.'

'Honest to God, I don't.'

'Well, anyway, I fecked the sugar and put it inside my blouse in a twist of paper. And that oul' Smullen spotted me. "Com'ere you, what's that you have. Give it here or I'll report you." "Feck off," I told him. It wasn't as if he was anyone. The next thing I knew, he had his hand down my neck, moryah* feeling for the sugar. Only it was my diddies he had hold of. You should have heard him. Panting as if he was having a fit. I nearly died! "I'll get you sacked," he kept saying, all the time he was rooting and pushing me up against the wall. And then he was fumbling with his trousers. "Hold this," he said and me like an eejit looks down and there was his mickey staring me in the face.'

'Sacred Heart of Jesus!' my mother exclaimed, making the sign of the cross. 'What did you do?'

'"Shove it up your arse and make a jug-handle," I shouted, and up with my knee leaving him not knowing if it was Monday or a Saturday. "You dirty oul' gouger." And by that time I didn't care whether I was sacked or not.'

My mother was laughing so much that she nearly cried.

'Oh, Molly, you're a terrible woman.' She dabbed at her eyes with the corner of her pinnie then went into another kink of laughing.

* Under the pretext of, from the Irish *mar dhea*.

I kept very quiet and hoped that my brother, who had fallen asleep, wouldn't waken and draw her attention. Enthralled by Molly's anecdotes she had forgotten all about me. But very soon she remembered and made faces to Molly to change the conversation. And so it was to be for many years. Everything, graphic descriptions of death agonies, the signs and symptoms of TB, breast amputations, murders, poisonings, the hanging and quartering of dead patriots, all were discussed in front of children, but never sex or how babies were born.

Sex had something to do with dirty things, that much I had deduced from my mother's warnings. Dirty things to do with boys and knickers. Young fellas must never see your knickers let alone pull them down. Straight to hell you went for anything like that, and into the bargain, she'd kill me. If anyone ever attempted to touch me I was to come home immediately and tell her.

Molly said that Mr Smullen was a head-buck-cat in the Men's Sodality but the holy ones were often the worst. Then she changed the conversation and told my mother about a girl they had both worked with who was now money-lending. After she left, my mother began talking to herself aloud. 'There's the answer to my prayer. St Jude didn't let me down. I'll be able to have my window-box; I know where to get the money.'

But during the next few days her mood swung between jubilation at the prospect of the money-lender and a way of borrowing the money and depression at the realization of what the transaction involved. Unlike the Jewman, Sarah wouldn't call for payments, but unlike the Jewman, Sarah didn't charge a fair rate of interest. Sarah was a daylight robber who'd lend two pounds on the condition that two pounds five shillings was returned to her once a week. Week after week she demanded the whole sum and the interest, so you were never out of her clutches. How could you be? How could any woman afford to say, 'Here's your money and the interest and I won't be wanting a lend anymore'?

It was a crying shame that poor women were obligated to the likes of Sarah. A big common heap who'd set up her money-lending on the strength of insurance collected on the head of someone dying. And you wouldn't mind if it was someone belonging to her. Probably some old man or woman she only knew by sight. But what did the society-men care who you insured so long as their books were full and the money paid regularly and a dab in the fist for them when the policy was cashed. Of course, if women didn't live in dread and fear of their husbands finding out they were in with a money-lender, the likes of Sarah couldn't do business. The threat of letting your husband know, that's what they held over you. Men never asked how you managed, how you put three meals a day on the table, dressed them and their children. But let it be known you were in with a money-lender and suddenly they wanted to know what you were doing with their wages. But talking wouldn't alter anything and in any case she had to have the window-box and blue velvet banner.

Once her mind was made up I was sent with a note and a penny for myself to the money-lender. In no time I was back with the two pound notes and being promised to secrecy. 'I'll let your father think I borrowed it from Maggie and let her believe he got me the money in tips. And if you breathe a word to either of them I'll cut the legs from under you. And tomorrow I'll get a neighbour to keep an eye on the other two and me and you'll go to the Iveagh Market and then into town and if you're good I'll buy you something for yourself.'

I woke early, full of excitement. I loved going into town with my mother. My father was good-humoured, explained things to me on our journeys into town, but there wasn't the magic about those outings that there was on my mother's. She knew so many people. Knew so much about everywhere we went. And though the information was forthcoming only in fits and starts and often interspersed with cross words and the promise of slaps when we got home, she made the streets and buildings come alive.

Crossing the Poddle where, she told me, there was an underground river, old women would call to her, 'Good morrow daughter.' She'd return their greetings and explain as they passed that they'd known her mother and her grandmother before that. On this morning she again drew my attention to the little park in Patrick Street and St Patrick's Cathedral. St Patrick, she said, had stood on that very spot. But that was years ago before the Protestants came and took it over. Every year it was sinking, inch by inch, into the ground. I wondered, as I often did, would I pass by one day and the Cathedral have vanished.

Once I saw a man in the park asleep on a bench wearing a red silk tie which lay on his bare chest. My mother said he was a poor unfortunate without a shirt on his back out of the Iveagh lodging-house, where at night, when all the beds were filled, men slept lying over a rope. And in the mornings the rope was cut. No wonder he was sleeping on the bench. It would be the poor night's rest leaning over a rope. Still, she supposed, it was better than sleeping in the street. He had Lord Iveagh to thank for that. He built the lodging-house. He'd made his money out of porter. But he gave some of it back. He built the Iveagh Buildings as well. Little dog-boxes that she wouldn't live in, not if she got one for nothing. And he built the Iveagh Market, too. Once upon a time the dealers sold second-hand clothes from the stones in Patrick Street, before the market was built. Some of them were wallowing in money, house property and everything. Though how they'd made it was another thing. One, she knew for a fact, made her fortune when a farmer, coming out of a public house in Patrick Street, dropped his handkerchief. There were hundreds, thousands, of sovereigns in it and quick as you like the oul' wan had it under her petticoat and the farmer mouldy drunk going around like a fool looking for it.

We cut through Back Lane and into Francis Street, where the market was. Above the door were carved heads. Strange-looking men with grey stone curls and beards. My mother said the one in the middle was supposed to be Lord Iveagh. Up the steps I followed her and into the noise and smell of disinfectant, old clothes and fruit from the adjoining market.

The dealers had their wares laid out, some on boards, the overflow in piles on the floor. Footwear of all sizes, shapes and description was lined in pairs. Suede, canvas and leather stained by sweat, moulded by misshapen feet. Their uppers, tongues and eyelets looking like old ugly faces, creased into grimaces as if they too had suffered the pain of the corns, bunions and ingrowing toe-nails. Gathered around each stall crowds of women watched and waited for an item of clothing or bedding they needed and could afford. We joined the group. 'Here y'are girls,' the dealer called, picking up and shaking out a pair of shrunken yellowed combinations. 'They'll keep the life in him. Who'll give me one and six, one and threepence? Ah, come on, won't one of youse give me a hansel?' There were no takers and the combs were thrown to the side. The dealer picked up a bundle of baby clothes. 'Look at these. You've all got little childer. Five bob. Outta a house in Ballsbridge. Who'll give me five bob, four and six, four shillings? What ails you? Are you all virgins. All sleeping with your two legs in the one stocking, what? Three and six and that's my last word.' A woman said she'd have them. The clothes were wrapped in a sheet of newspaper and the money went into the dealer's enormous apron pocket.

I pulled on my mother's hand impatient to get out of the crowd, hemmed in by the jostling women, my view of the dealer and her stall being obscured. 'You behave yourself or I'll rosen your jaw,' my mother said in a voice that only I could hear. We left the group and I breathed in a big breath of the bruised orange smell. 'I'll give it to you when I get you home,' she continued as we went towards the side stalls from where she bought her antiques.

She admired a framed picture of Kathleen Mavourneen, with verses of the song printed inside lozenge-shapes decorating Kathleen's head and shoulders. The shelves and tables overflowed with stuffed animals and wax fruit beneath glass shades. The centrepiece was a pair of snowy owls which fixed me with their stare and made me keep close to my mother. Blackened silver-topped cruets and inkstands, inlaid writing boxes, copper kettles and velvet-framed photographs of stout men and women leaning against flower-trailed trellises and Grecian urns, all were on display.

'I have another one of them books—I kept it for you,' the stallholder said. 'It's a grand story about a little girl and her grandfather. 'Little Nell'—I don't know if you've ever read it.' He reached under the table and brought out the book. 'Fourpence,' he said.

'All right.' My mother never bargained for books. 'But wait'll I tell you. I'm looking for a curtain-pole about this long.' She held her arms apart to show the size. 'I'm making a banner for the window. For the Eucharistic Congress, you know.'

'I've got the very thing. Hold on now.' He went to look and came back with an armful of curtain-poles.

'They'd all be too big,' my mother said measuring them with her eye.

'You could saw a lump off.'

'What are you asking?'

'Seven shillings each—they're mahogany, and the rings thrown in.'

'Sure I'd have to cut one nearly in half and mahogany's awful

45

hard to cut. Four bob.'

'I couldn't part with them for less than six.'

'Come on,' my mother said catching my hand, preparing to walk away, banking on him calling her back.

'Listen ma'am, com'ere. Make it five and a tanner and I'll throw in the book as well.'

'All I have is four and six.'

'God, you're a terrible woman,' the man said in mock sorrow.

'Shaggin' oul' robber! He'd have got them in a lot for nothing,' my mother said as she manoeuvred the pole out through the market.

'You never bought me anything,' I complained as we came into Christchurch Place.

Ignoring my complaint, as she frequently did, my mother was telling me about the neighbourhood we were passing through. 'Do you see there—the other side of Michael's Hill? Well years ago one of them shops sold coffins. Lined up outside the door, you could buy one the way you'd buy a loaf of bread or a stone of coal. And there was this oul' wan and her cronies short of funds for a drink. And she let on to be dead. They bought a coffin, on score. She was laid out and everything and they got the society money. Only she was found out. They left her too long in the coffin while everyone else was admiring her and drinking porter. I believe there was ructions once they got over the fright of her sitting up in the coffin and calling them a lot of mean oul' cows.'

We went down Winetavern Street and along the quays. I wanted to cross the road and look down at the Liffey. There was nothing to see, my mother said. There was the water and sometimes swans and Guinness boats going down to the North Wall and, if the tide was out, seagulls walking in the mud round the edge. There was plenty to see. But we kept walking on the other side. Sometimes stopping to look in the windows of the shops that sold statues and rosaries and holy pictures. Then on we went down to McBirney's where bales of material lay shelved from floor to ceiling and hung in swathes from stands. All the colours of the rainbow, patterns of flowers, stripes, circles, dots, pin-stripes, chalkstripes, textures as soft as down, as rough as heather. Satins and silks, art-silks and shantung, taffeta and tweed. Voiles and georgette, crêpe and tussore, linen and gingham, crash and canvas, linings and leatherette, wools and worsteds, velvets and velours. The colours of sand and biscuits, cream and raspberries, coffee and chocolate, lilacs and red roses, sugar-stick and virgin blue, emerald green, sugar-bag blue, grey like wet slates, yellows like lemons and paler yellows like country butter. My mother inspected the velvets for the shade she wanted. Decided, changed her mind, went to another bale, felt the pile, checked on the width and price, hesitated, then made up her mind and went to the counter. I watched the assistants binding bales on the counter, racing out material, smoothing it, cutting, folding and wrapping; writing dockets, taking the money, reaching above their heads where, with a flick of the wrist, they undid little boxes suspended from wires running between the counters and the cashier's office. The little boxes resembled stud cases, the bottom half unscrewed leaving the top attached to the wires. Into it was placed the money and docket. Then with another wrist movement the halves were joined and sent zooming along to the office, returning in the same fashion with receipts and change. My mother talked to the assistant telling her about the banner—the design she intended working on it in gold braid. The assistant said it sounded great and when she measured the braid gave my mother the few inches left on the card for nothing. 'A little lady,' was how she described the assistant as we left the shop. We went home by a different route. I was glad her arms were full so that she had no free hand with which to push me between the shoulder blades and tell me to walk straight. Westmoreland Street was full of the smell of Bewley's coffee. I sniffed and looked into their window at the assortment of cakes.

'Can we go in?' I asked.

'No,' my mother said, 'Bewley's is too dear. I'll buy you something later on.'

In Camden Street white-aproned, black-shawled dealers were selling fish, fruit and flowers. My mother bought bananas from a rosy-cheeked dealer with black hair and very white teeth. When we left the stall my mother said she was a fine woman and that my father knew her well, sometimes they drank together in a pub in Camden Street. Sometimes he borrowed money from the dealer until the weekend. But she was a decent woman and as old if not older than herself. In a shop farther up the street she bought me sheets of scraps—lacquered paper shapes of cherubic

47

children, baskets of fruit and flowers and gorgeous kittens and pups. The scraps had a shiny surface and a lovely smell. The perforations came easily apart. Already I was beginning to separate them. 'Give them here to me or you'll have them blowing all over the road,' my mother said. At home I would finish the separating, store them in a lesson book and in school swop the ones I had duplicates of.

My mother hid the curtain-pole underneath the bed and the velvet and braid amongst bedclothes in the press. Not for a while would she let my father and Maggie know about them. When eventually she did, my father admired everything and asked how she had managed to buy them. Maggie, she told him, had lent her the money and said there was no hurry about paying it back. Maggie, when she was shown the makings of the banner and heard that my father had provided the money said, 'Well, with all his faults he has the redeeming of them.'

In the evenings my mother measured and cut and sewed, good humoured, singing snatches of songs and when satisfied that she had done enough, read me fairy tales and promised that when I was older she would read me 'Little Nell'.

The velvet was lined with blue art-silk and its edges trimmed with the gold braid. In its centre she entwined the braid to form the letters I.H.S. and found a fellow to shorten the pole and make the window-boxes. The room smelled of bark and the moss, earth and plants with which the boxes were filled.

In the weeks that followed, my mother agonized over the Lindbergh baby. 'The poor unfortunate child. May God comfort his parents. How could any mother or father stay sane not knowing where their child was or if they would ever see it again.'

My father regretted that he hadn't bought a ticket for the Irish Sweep. The draw was to take place soon. My mother forgot for the moment about the Lindbergh baby and fantasized about what she would do if she won the Sweep, and whether, if next year she had a ticket and drew a horse, she would sell the ticket.

'But imagine if you did and then the horse won, wouldn't you be killing yourself after handing over your chance for a couple of hundred and the horse coming in first?'

'It's all a gamble,' my father said. 'Everything depends on luck.'

'Would you never take him with you this morning?' my mother said to him one Sunday.

'No,' my father said. 'I did last Sunday and every time anyone spoke to him he wouldn't open his mouth.'

'Not every child is as full of affectation as that one.' I didn't care that my mother thought I was a shaper or that my brother wasn't coming. I liked it better going on my own.

'It's all because you have him clinging to your skirts,' my father said. And my brother scowled, dropped his chin on his chest then buried his face in my mother's skirt.

'Well, and where did you go?' my mother asked when we came home later on.

'To the Botanic Gardens,' I answered truthfully. For a long time now my father hadn't taken me to the sweet shop.

***

The Lindbergh baby was found dead near his parents' home; the Sweepstake was drawn and Primo Carnera was boxing in Dalymount Park and then everyone's thoughts were directed to the Eucharistic Congress at the end of June. Fine weather was prayed for and work began on the site in the Phoenix Park where the main celebration was to take place. Thousands of people would come to Dublin. The Papal Legate, bishops and cardinals from all the Catholic countries in the world. A special altar was being constructed in O'Connell Street where the Papal Legate would celebrate mass. Special trains and buses were being laid on to bring people from all over Ireland to Dublin. In the street bunting was hung and window-boxes bloomed. My mother wouldn't hang out her banner until the night before the beginning of the celebrations for fear someone might copy her design.

My father laughed at her and said it would be a bit late in the day for anyone to do that. 'All the same,' she replied, 'it's not going out until the last minute.'

On the night the banner was to be hung she waited for my father to come home and he didn't. She consoled herself that maybe a late removal had come in. A foreign visitor could have dropped dead in a hotel. And hotels wouldn't have a body removed in daylight. So he was working late. She put the other children to bed but let me stay up. 'He'll be here in a minute,' she kept saying each time she went to the window for a sign of him. 'But what'll I do about the banner if he isn't?' The man who had made the window-boxes had fixed a ring to the window-sill to hold the banner's pole and as the night wore on she wondered if she could manage to slip the pole in herself. 'I'll wait a bit longer,' she said and made tea for the two of us. Afterwards she put out the gas, wrapped a rug around me and we sat by the window looking out into the street. Every so often she'd say, 'Ahhh, I think that's him now.' But the footsteps came nearer and the person into view and it wasn't him.

'Will we go to the park?' I asked her.

'Yes,' she said but I knew she wasn't really listening to me and she began talking aloud to herself. 'What'll I do? I've left it too late to ask them next door. There's not a sound from there. They're all in bed. Not that I'd want them to know my business. But if he doesn't come in or is face falling, I won't get the banner up. And I wanted it flying before morning.' Then she told me to come away from the window. She lit the gas again. 'I'll have to do it myself,' she said and pushed up the window. The cold night air blew into the room. 'You stay by the fire, I don't want you to get your end,' she said as she manoeuvred the pole and its banner out through the window. 'The curse of hell on that fella; I know he didn't shave enough off the end.' She kept talking to herself as she struggled and pushed. 'Get me the hammer outta your father's tool-box. No don't. Sure I wouldn't be able to reach the top of the pole to hit it. Wait now. I'll pull it in again. Don't you move from the fire.' She hauled in the pole and laid it on the floor and got the big carving-knife, sharp as a razor, its edge worn to a dagger-like point and began hacking at the bottom of the pole. 'I'll try it again,' she said and this time she succeeded in wedging the pole into its ring. 'Three o'clock in the morning—where is he till this hour? Wait'll he comes in, I'll give it to him.' I was too tired to care whether she did or not. 'Shh,' she said, 'That's him. Get into bed you. And don't let on to be awake.'

I never heard my father come in and in the morning was too sick to know or care if they had rowed. I had the measles. Plastered with them, my mother said. She gave me saffron tea and kept the curtains drawn so that I wouldn't go blind. My father assured her that the banner was the best in the street. And she said, 'No thanks to you.' Right through the week of the Eucharistic Congress I seemed to sleep at any opportunity, and never saw our church floodlit or went into O'Connell Street to see the decorations, nor to the Phoenix Park where thousands of children, dressed in white and wearing veils, went to mass.

Everyone, so my mother said, had told her her window display was the best in the street. Even my aunt Maggie admitted that the banner was a picture, but added that there were few streets where the people hadn't shone with their decorations, the loveliest altars and flags and bunting and flowers. It was no wonder that one of the English papers had written, 'Dublin's poor are Dublin's rich in the eyes of the world tonight.' You could leave it to a Dubliner to show how things were done.

She wanted to know if my mother had found out where my father had been until three o'clock in the morning. 'According to him,' my mother said, 'playing cards in some fella's house.'

'I hope you asked him if he thought there was any green in your eye?'

'He was too drunk. Asleep before I knew it. And the next day she had the measles and I was run off my feet. All the plans I had came to nothing. I saw none of it. But thank God she's overed them without any complications. And the flower-boxes will last through the summer.'

'You're an awful geish swallowing that story about a card school. He's carrying on with someone—you mark my words. If he was my husband I'd swing for him.'

'Well, he isn't so keep your advice till I ask for it.'

The banner was taken down. 'It'll come in handy for something,' my mother said, looking at her handiwork, then smoothing it, folding it and putting it away. Each week I went to the money-lender with two pound notes and two half-crowns, my mother saying as she folded the money into my palm, 'I hope to Jesus she won't close her hand on me this week.' Throughout the summer I went with the payments, until one day my mother sat down and with a pencil on the back of a brown paper bag, did some calculations.

'The daylight robber,' she said when she'd finished. 'She's more than well paid. Not another farthing will she handle from me. Not if she came and read the riot act in the middle of the road or accosted your father and told him.' Then she put on her hat and coat and went to the money-lender's from where she returned dancing with joy. Only sorry that she could relate her victory to no one but me.

'She won't forget my visit in a hurry. The robber. A heap of commonality. "Sarah," sez I to her, "do you know when I got the loan from you?" "I do," sez she, "I keep a note of my transactions." "Then in that case you'll know you've been paid over and over again and you'll never handle another penny of mine." I took the wind out of her sails. "And another thing, don't think for a minute that you can browbeat me by threatening to tell my husband for he knows all about it." "God Aggie," sez she, "you don't think I'd be guilty of such a thing." The bloody liar! Anyway, I left her dropping. I gave her her character and told her there should be a law against the likes of her. I wish you could have seen her face. It's only a pity I didn't do what I did sooner.'

With the relief of the loan behind her, the fine weather, and the fact that my father was coming home early and seldom going out in the evenings, she was happy and good-humoured most of the time.

SIX

Periodically, letters came from America and occasionally from my English grandfather. 'The mean oul' bastard,' my mother would say after a quick look to see if he had sent anything, 'and him wallowing in it.' She shook the envelope in case notes or a cheque had lodged inside. 'Not a brown ha'penny—and after all you did for him. Working in his office for nothing, and me, like a three-quarter-bred-thick, sending him that lovely cravat from Galligan's in Dame Street. But sure, what could you expect from an oul' fella that sold the house from under you lock, stock and barrel when your mother died, with all her things in it and your books and school prizes. The oul' shite.'

But despite my grandfather's parsimonious ways my mother always encouraged my father to keep in touch with him. For, as she said, you never knew in the long run—when he died you might come in for it all. In the meantime there were the American airmail envelopes that seldom came without dollars which my mother used to extricate herself from her most pressing debts, and to buy more antiques and toys for us. An enormous dilapidated rocking-horse which, she said, with a lick of paint, a new saddle and reins and its mangey tail and mane renewed, would be as good as if it had come out of a toyshop. My father did the renovating and before our delighted eyes the horse became a beauty.

From the next windfall I had a coach-built doll's pram. Like the horse it needed restoration which my mother, with deft fingers, immeasurable patience, wadding and American cloth, tackled and completed. In the pram my baby doll forever slept unless I tilted the pillow. I was in ecstasies pushing the pram to and fro, dressing and undressing the doll, arranging the pillow and coverlet. My brother, in a cowboy hat with holster and cap pistols, galloped his horse. Faster and faster he rode across imagined prairies, the rockers pounding the floor, until my mother's temper snapped and the horse was threatened with destruction. A similiar fate awaited the pram and I was to go at once and get her a Setziller Powder for her sick headache.

Back with the powder in its blue paper, I watched her mix it in a tumbler of water and heard her complain that there wasn't room to move, never mind accommodate that gazebo of a horse. She must have been out of her mind to buy it and her living in one room. And what possessed her to bring in a doll's pram when there wasn't enough room for a real one? Before you knew it the baby would be walking. Falling over each other we'd be. How that poor unfortunate creature on the landing managed with nine of them in a dog-box, she didn't know. First thing in the morning she would be down to Lord Edward Street about a house. And along with her novena to St Jude light a lamp in John's Lane to the Mother of Good Counsel.

But summer was coming and soon her faith in miracles would be restored and with it her humour. All the days were summer then. Women walked out in their figures. The tar melted on the road and red, white and black currants, their tart juices delightful on your tongue, were sold in pennyworths, as were soft, rosy, hairy gooseberries, full of seeds and sweetness. My mother whitened my runners with pipeclay and put them on the window-sill to dry. They were brought in dazzling white, smelling of hot canvas and rubber. They were like wings on my feet. The whitening, where it had been applied too thickly, cracked and fell in flakes.

I ran to call my friends. 'Someone's playing chainies in the haggard', the word went round. Soon a trail of little girls carrying cardboard boxes were making their way to the tussocky field behind Fleming's dairy yard. A field full of bees and buttercups, clover and daisies, butterflies and brambles. Here we set up our shops to play chainies. Chainies were played with pieces of broken china, delft, glass and earthenware collected from dustbins, homes and anyone who would give them to you. Large flat stones in ones or twos, with a plank or a sturdy piece of cardboard balanced on them, were used as counters. Sheets of newspapers were torn into squares and dexterously wound round small fingers to make three-cornered bags. The stock was set out. Sprigged, fine pieces of china sold as expensive sweets. Brown earthenware masqueraded as dripping, green porter-bottle-glass was labelled jallop.* For money we used white golden-trimmed china, the half-cups, smashed saucers and plates taken from dustbins, broken further into varying-sized pieces to match as nearly as possible shillings, half-crowns, sixpences and threepenny bits.

Like antique dealers we went from stall to stall inspecting the wares, envious of dealers with a larger stock of the pretty flower-strewn fragments. Then our shops were declared open and for hours we bought and sold. Haggling over prices, refusing to serve anyone who criticized our lay-out or with whom we had an ongoing quarrel. Getting furious if a customer leant too heavily on our makeshift counters; and when it was time to go home we packed up our shops in cardboard boxes and promised each other we would play chainies tomorrow.

Sometimes we did and sometimes we didn't, for there were many pleasant pastimes to occupy us during the summer holidays. Outings to St Stephen's Green only a short walk from the street, with ducks to feed and enormous-seeming fields of grass to run in. Beds of flowers that looked and smelled gorgeous; fountains with water dancing in the air, falling in cascades of crystal drops. And all the people! Beautiful people. Women in silky, flowing, swirling dresses. Children with heads of glossy ringlets and wide satin ribbons tying them up in big bows. We ran and raced across the lawns, tunnelled through the dark laurel shrubberies, imagining ourselves on great adventures, conjuring visions of the things that any minute might confront us. We drank from the spouting mouths of lions, rolled and tumbled down the slight inclines, twirling over and over in the summer grass.

Then there were other days when I took my sister out in her pram, with my friend and her baby sister. 'Don't go any further than Harold's Cross Park and don't go on the swings,' my mother would say as she got the baby ready, made bread and jam and poured milk into an empty sauce-bottle whose neck she stopped with a wad of paper. To get to the park you had to pass the hospice. There was a tree near the deadhouse, where, so it

* Any unpleasant-tasting medicine.

55

was said, you saw the devil if you ran round it backwards three times. We never went to the park without visiting the hospice. A metal arch spanned its gates and worked into it in big letters were the words OUR LADY'S HOSPICE FOR THE DYING. Fearfully, I pushed the pram under the arch thinking of sick people passing beneath it, knowing they were going to die. Up the drive I pushed the pram, past the primary school and the pool of still, dark-green water where the rushes grew thickly, hoping we wouldn't meet a nun who would put us out. Hoping we would, and hoping we wouldn't see the devil after running round the tree. Hoping that the deadhouse would be empty, which it never was. On marble slabs with hollowed pillows to match, the bodies lay dressed in brown habits, sometimes with pennies on their eyes, their yellow fingers entwined in rosary beads.

I went from slab to slab morbidly fascinated, staring at the faces, aware all the time of the peculiar smell which I tried to liken to some other. There was nothing—except perhaps tulips. Tulips when they were fully blown. So tulips and chrysanthemums are associated in my mind with death. The round of the slabs completed there was nothing else to see, so I blessed myself and pushed my sister in her go-cart out into the sunshine. Once again we ran round the devil's tree but he never materialized and so we adjourned to Harold's Cross Park and the swings on which I was forbidden to swing. Soon, to the chant of, 'Die, die, little dog die', with a high swing and a low swing I was soaring up towards the blue sky, all thoughts of death far from my mind.

In the summer there was also the prospect of a day at the seaside. 'Wait'll we get a fine day and we'll go out to Blackrock,' my mother would say once May was passed, sometimes even going so far as to name a day which, when it arrived, more often than not wasn't the day we were going to the seaside, for one unexplained reason or another.

'But you promised,' I would say.

And she'd reply, 'Promises are made to be broken.' However, there were occasions when we did go and the announcement that this was the day created a feverish state of excitement. My mother searching out the woollen bathing togs, dispatching me to the pork butcher for cold ham and brawn. Me pleading for roast pork and being ordered to do what I was told, followed by an explanation that pork wasn't in season and in any case she didn't like it. Pigs, like mackerel, were scavengers and ate anything, including dead bodies. Sandwiches were made and bottles of water brought for the baby, a note left for my father, the dinner prepared for the evening and at last we were off, first by bus to Westland Row and then out by train to Blackrock.

All day the sun shone and the water was warm and the bladderwrack full and popped when I burst it. Every time I ventured farther into the sea than my ankles, my mother appeared with warnings of how easily you could be swept out and drowned.

There was sand in the bread and butter, it crunched under my teeth. The jelly round the brawn melted, soaking into the bread. I minded the baby while my mother went up to the little hut that sold refreshments. She came back with a jug of tea and two bottles of minerals. Everything tasted delicious.

In the afternoon a crowd of boys came down to the beach. They raced around, ran in and out of the water, splashing my mother who was carrying the baby while she paddled. 'You crowd of young curs,' she said, when after asking them to play elsewhere they thumbed their noses at her. 'If you don't shift this minute I'll call a policeman.'

The tide was going out, exposing more and more bladderwrack, the rocks were green and slimy and forbidden territory. The margin of sand became greater, plenty of wet sand on which to play with our buckets and spades, filling and smoothing the pails, upending them, beating their bottoms with our spades and chanting, 'Pie, pie come out, I owe you half a clout.' Then all too soon it was time to go home. With sand in our shoes, between our toes, in our mouths and hair we climbed the steps. Tired and sunburned and happy I licked my arms to cool the sting of the sun and tasted salt. 'It's been a grand day,' my mother would say. 'And one day we'll do it again, please God.'

SEVEN

Next summer I would be seven, able to know right from wrong, capable of distinguishing what sin was and old enough therefore to make my first communion. Preparation for receiving the sacrament of penance and Holy Communion began well in advance. Daily instruction was given by an old sweet-tempered nun who suffered from the cold so that even when pale spring sunshine flooded the classroom and the fire burned, she wore a soft woollen shawl and black fingerless mittens. 'There are so many sins,' she said. 'Quarrelling with your brothers and sisters, back answering your parents, forgetting to say your prayers, taking a ha'penny from your mother's purse, missing mass, impure thoughts and actions. Every one of them a sin—some venial, some mortal and every one of them must be confessed. Your soul died when you committed a mortal sin and if you died before confessing it God would send you straight to hell. Or if you went to confession and deliberately did not confess the mortal sin the same thing could happen—straight to hell you go. Only the sacrament of penance can save you. Only a good confession. In confession you must tell everyone of your sins. The most terrible thing that any person can do is to deliberately not confess a mortal sin and then receive the Blessed Sacrament. That is a sacrilege. For that you go to hell. Remember that children.'

She paused to adjust the shawl around her shoulders, then asked, 'What happens to anyone who commits a sacrilege?'

'They'll go to hell, Sister,' forty voices chorused.

'Indeed they will.' The nun nodded her head and the long hair which grew out of a mole on her chin waved like an antenna. I watched it and knew that if I died hell was waiting for me. For I had a terrible sin that I could never confess. A sin so awful that I could never bring myself to utter words to describe it, especially to a priest. Last summer in the haggard behind a bush I had pulled down my knickers and let a boy look at me, and afterwards watched him undo his few buttons and looked at him. Then we rearranged our clothes and played mothers and fathers. After he had bounced on me for a few times he said, 'That's the end of that game. Don't let on we played it or we'll be kilt.'

All through the months of preparation for my first communion the sin weighed heavily on my mind. For I knew that when the day came to confess, I wouldn't, and would receive the sacrament not in a state of grace. Then after committing the sacrilege I might be knocked down and killed. Or I could get fever and be taken to hospital. My mind flew off on its flight of fancy. I was lying dead on the road; lying in the fever hospital. Visitors looked at me through the glass partition, brought me bags of grapes and apples half-wrapped in soft tissue paper, bottles of minerals. My mother stood by my body on the road crying because I was dead. I was dead and going down to hell.

'And what will it be?' The nun's voice brought me back to reality. 'The happiest day of your life, Sister,' answered the class. 'The happiest day of your life,' repeated the old nun. 'Napoleon said that. A great man, a famous French man, like a king nearly. When someone asked him what had been the happiest day of his life, that's what he replied. The day he made his first Holy Communion. Imagine that! With all his honours and all the great battles he had won, that was the day he remembered as the happiest in his life.' In the corridor the bell rang. 'Now let us say our afternoon prayers and then go quietly home.'

Outside there were many things to distract my mind from sin and sacrilege. Seagulls screaming and swooping in the playground, searching for crusts of bread dropped at lunchtime. The slope to run down and the money wrapped in a piece of rag tucked up the leg of my knickers with which to buy 'taffee'. And if it was a Thursday, the slaughterhouse where the cows that had run frantically down the street in the morning were being killed.

I lay on the cobbles and looked through the gap in the big wooden door. The sheep and cows moved restlessly in their pens. I turned my eyes this way and that as far as they would go but never saw an animal being killed. Only pools of blood, entrails, and stained fleeces being loaded onto a cart.

One afternoon when I came home from school my mother announced that I was to have lizard-skin shoes when I made my communion. 'But I wanted white buckskin with a strap.'

'Lizard is very uncommon—no one else will have them.'

'I want white ones, soft buckskin with a strap the same as everyone, please, please.'

'You'll wear what I say,' my mother dismissed my pleas and went on to describe the dress my aunt was making me. It was a crêpe-de-Chine, full-length with a picot-edged frill at the hem and a bunch of baby-ribbon at the waist. 'And I'm getting you a crocheted mob-cap as well.'

'I want a wreath with little flowers and leaves—the same as the one we saw. You said I could have that. You promised.'

But my mother, having decided that a mob-cap and lizard shoes would lift me out of the crowd, was deaf to my pleadings.

* * *

'Bless me Father, for I have sinned and this is my first confession. I told lies, I was disobedient and forgot my morning prayers. I hit my brother and back answered my mother. For these and all my sins I am sorry.'

'For your penance say three Hail Marys.'

It was over—I had made my confession and deliberately omitted the terrible sin. I tip-toed out of the box and devoutly, on quaking legs, walked to the altar to say my penance, expecting every moment that from somewhere above me a voice would thunder, 'You never told the worst sin. You can't receive in the morning. You'll commit a sacrilege if you do.'

In the dim light, kneeling before the altar, surrounded by statues of angels and saints, relics, and flickering penny candles, their smoke ascending heavenwards, I was terrified of hell. And I knew the devil was sitting on my left shoulder laughing gleefully. Quickly I said the second-half of the Confiteor and the three Hail Marys.

But once in the chapel yard, being assembled into line, two by two, the fear and foreboding was replaced by thoughts of tomorrow, the new clothes I would wear and all the excitement of visiting relations. I kept thinking of myself dressed in the gorgeous clothes. Every stitch brand new. I had already handled them and smelled their newness—even the hated shoes, grey and rough-textured, with flakes of black ingrained in the leather. Horrible, horrible shoes, but I hoped the frill of my dress would hide them. My handbag was white crêpe and beaded. Tomorrow friends, neighbours and relations would fill it with money. And after receiving my communion I was going to have breakfast with my aunt. It would be a marvellous day.

The nun marched us back to school, where before being dismissed, she reminded us that tomorrow would be the happiest day of our lives. One we would remember always. A day when our souls were spotless. Pure enough to receive the body and blood of our Lord Jesus Christ. Then she walked down the line touching each child, telling us to go quietly home, not to break our fast after supper and above all commit no sin between now and morning. And tomorrow, when we received the precious body of Christ, on no account let it touch our teeth. If we couldn't swallow it at once, leave it on our tongue to dissolve.

My vest, knickers, petticoat and socks were laid out on the fireguard. My mother warmed water, stood me on a chair and washed me all over, for you had to be spotless in the body as well as soul. On a hanger was the dress, picot-edged and ribbon-bedecked and around its shoulders the veil, shorter than I would have liked, but lovely all the same, and on the chair the hated shoes.

'Thank God you have a lovely day for it,' my mother said as she rubbed the soapy cloth over my face and as usual got soap in my eyes. Not even the prospect of being decked in all my grandeur reduced the stinging smart. Tears and stuping with cold water dulled the pain and I was attired. The delightful sensation of the new clothes touching my body, the softness of the knickers and vest, the whiteness of them, the tiny ribbon threaded through the neck of the vest fastening it with the smallest bow imaginable, the silkiness of the hand-made socks. 'You're a picture,' my mother said when she was satisfied that my hair was to her liking. From its top to its tip, between finger and thumb, she gently pulled my nose. 'Do that every morning,' she said, 'and you'll grow up to have an aristocratic nose. Now, step into your dress.' It floated about me, the skirt buoyant over the in-built petticoats. The picot-edged frill stood out. It was the most glorious thing I had ever worn. 'Your hair is tossed. Com'ere till I do it again.' I was combed and brushed and the veil arranged on my head and then the mob-cap—I think it had ear muffs. I'm sure it had ear muffs. 'Look at yourself,' my mother said, holding out the mirror. The cap spoiled everything. My face stared out, sullen-looking, my brown fringe bound by the crochet silk, the muffs hanging like elephants' ears. 'Hold on to the table while I put on your shoes.' I balanced on one leg and the shoe was forced onto my foot. 'Them socks are not the ones you were wearing when you tried on the shoes—they were a grand fit then. Hold still and stop squirming.'

'They're hurting me.'

'They'll stretch by the time you get to the chapel.'

Small girls dressed like miniature brides sat on one side of the chapel; on the other, small boys in short-trousered suits, serges and tweeds, navys, blues, fawns, and browns, newly shod and wearing three-quarter-length socks. There was music and singing. Light-headed with excitement and hunger, I said the prayers I had been taught to say before receiving. Soon we would be given the signal to approach the altar. Hand in hand with my little partner I would walk devoutly up the aisle, kneel at the rail and raise the starched cloth to beneath my chin. And the priest would come gliding towards me along the altar steps, murmuring in Latin. My tongue would be out waiting. I felt very hot, then cold and clammy. Maybe I was going to faint. If I fainted I couldn't commit a sacrilege. I'd be carried out, sat on a chair in the porch. They'd have to give me a glass of water. My fast would be broken—I couldn't receive. I was going to faint. I could feel myself swaying, stars before my eyes. I was, I was going to faint. Then Hannah nudged me. It was the turn of our line. The girls at the front of the seat were rising. Hannah was taking my hand. I was standing, inching along, out in the aisle, walking to the altar. I put out my tongue and waited. The host was placed upon it. Nothing happened except that I thought it tasted like an ice-cream biscuit. With joined hands and bent head I went back to my seat and knelt to pray. The host wasn't dissolving. It had stuck to the roof of my mouth, my tongue reached and dislodged it, it touched my teeth and automatically I chewed and swallowed. On the happiest day of my life I had already committed two grievous sins.

But outside the sun was shining and in the chapel yard women came and admired my dress, lifted the hem and admired my petticoats and told me I looked lovely and my mother that I was a credit to her. Thoughts of sin were banished as I revelled in the praise and attention. Mothers and children began to drift away. Hunger now was uppermost in my mind. I hadn't eaten or drunk anything for more than twelve hours. I wanted to go to my aunt's—I wanted my breakfast.

The usual Sunday breakfast was served to me as a special treat. I gorged on delicious fried bacon, sausages, black and white pudding, bread fried to a pale golden crispness and eggs with their yolks basted to perfection.

By the time I returned home the lizard shoes were rubbing my heels.

'You'll have to break them in,' my mother said when I complained about them.

'I can't. They're hurting me.'

'You'll have to put up with them, your father will be in in a minute to take you to visit his relations. And you can't go all done up in your communion clothes with your old shoes. Give them here and I'll rub a bit of soap on the clicks.'

I slipped out of the shoes and my mother soaped the backs of them. For a while they didn't hurt so much.

By the time the visiting of my father's relations was finished my communion bag was weighted with money, my heels rubbed raw and my socks stained crimson from the broken blisters. 'It's not far for the bus, try to think about something else and it won't hurt so much,' my father said as we walked through Merrion Square. I was limping and feeling miserable and thinking how far it was to the bus and how I could never walk that far when suddenly my father stopped and I looked at him and saw that his face was the colour of chalk. 'Oh, God,' he said, 'if only there was somewhere to sit down.'

Thinking it was the state of my heels that concerned him I said, 'That's what I want to do, sit down and take off my shoes.'

'You can't go in the park love, unless you live on the square and have a key.'

I noticed then that he was breathing strangely, panting. He stopped and leant against the park railings, taking big breaths, pushing his hat to the back of his head, loosening his tie and I realized there was something wrong with him. He slid down the railings and crouched on the small stone base. Taking out his handkerchief he wiped his face of sweat. I sat beside him and held his hand tight and after what seemed like a long time he gave a big sigh and said, 'Well, whatever it was it's gone now.' Slowly he stood up. 'Yes, I'm alright now. Did I give you a fright?' I nodded. 'It was nothing. Rushing around, that's all it was. I'm fine now. But I'll have to do something about your shoes. Sit down and take them off.' The shoes were stuck by the blood to my socks. My father knelt before me and gently eased them off. 'I know how I'll fix them. You just sit there.' From his pocket he took out a packet of Players, emptied the cigarettes into his hand. 'Here,' he said, 'squash them in on top of your money.' Then he made two wads of the packet and placed one in each shoe. 'That'll raise your heels so that the shoes don't rub. It'll last until we get to the bus.'

He stood up and fixed his hat and tie.

'Come on love, we'll go home.'

I was delighted because he didn't look sick any more. When we got home he told my mother he had felt weak, as if he was going to faint.

'A touch of malaria, I think it was.'

She was counting my communion money, making little piles of the halfcrowns, two shilling pieces, sixpenny bits and the very few coppers.

'I thought you had to have gone foreign to get malaria,' she said.

'There's mosquitoes everywhere. What else could it have been?'

'Drink maybe?' suggested my mother.

'I never wet my lips. Will you go up to the chemist and get me a dose of quinine? Here,' he said giving her a ten shilling note, 'get a few sweets for yourself and the children.'

My mother gave me two shillings and the coppers from my communion money and put the rest in her bag. Later, when I was in bed, I listened to them talking. Heard my father describe the terrible weakness that had come over him. 'Every ounce of strength drained from my body. I was sure I was going to faint. It wouldn't have mattered if I'd been on my own but I was worrying about her.' My mother assured him that it was nothing—the change in the weather maybe. Millions of things could make you faint. It was definitely nothing to worry about.

I thought about my sacrilege. God became very angry when you offended him; maybe that's why my father had nearly fainted. God knew I loved my father more than anyone in the whole world. And He was punishing me.

By Monday he was completely recovered and went to work. The lizard-skin shoes went into the pawn and I hoped would never come out again. In school we were congratulated on having made our Holy Communion and reminded that from now on we must be more careful than ever before doing anything to offend Almighty God. Though he didn't look ill after his bad turn my father developed a short dry cough. My mother administered tarry-smelling cough medicine and doses of criticism and advice. 'What other way could your health be with you staying out half the night. Mixing with God only knows who. Sleep and rest you need, plenty of it. I only hope you won't live to regret whatever it is you're doing. That it won't be the cause of destroying your constitution.'

To my aunt she confided that she smelt a rat—there was something going on. Two or three nights a week he came home at all hours. And the funny thing was there was no sign of drink.

'I warned you, didn't I? Have you searched his pockets.'

'Once or twice,' said my mother, 'but it's not easy in the one room. In any case I found nothing.'

'Then you'll have to folly him.'

'He'd kill me if he found out.'

'Then make sure he doesn't. One night when you know he's going out, get Kitty to keep an eye on the children. Have it arranged beforehand. Then let him go. Give him five minutes—then dog him.'

My mother acted on her sister's advice but the manoeuvre came to nothing. 'I was going great,' she related to my aunt. 'Keeping my distance, dodging into doorways if he showed signs of looking round, but never losing sight of him. Then do you know what he did?'

'No,' said my aunt.

'He only jumped on a bus. So what else could I do but come home?'

There was an uneasy atmosphere. My mother was preoccupied to such an extent she seldom listened to anything I said. She was even too disinterested in what went on—the quarrel between myself and my brother, people coming in to use the yard, my father's untidiness—to lose her temper. It was all very strange. And the special treat of reading us bedtime stories became a thing of the past.

But there was always my adored cat Woolley who, since the baby doll had fallen from the table and smashed her china head, allowed herself to be dressed in the doll's clothes and lay contentedly in my pram with her paws resting on the apron. I adored her, her beautifully marked fur, her creamy belly, sharp needle-pointed teeth and pink clean rough tongue. When I nursed her I could feel the beat of her heart. She stretched and reached a paw to touch my face. One Saturday afternoon Woolley didn't come for her dinner. A search was started on the stairs and landing, under the stairs, in the yard and the outhouse. My father and I went making the noise she answered to. By this time I was crying for my lost cat. 'Maybe she was run over,' I sobbed and we looked in the street, along the gutters. But she wasn't anywhere.

'I'll have a last look in the yard before it gets dark,' my father said. I followed him in and watched him climb up on the wall.

'She might,' he said, 'be down there in Yodaikens,' looking into the big yard at the rear of our house. He climbed over and returned carrying the body of Woolley. By this time my mother had joined us in the yard.

'Is she dead?' she asked.

'No, but she's very sick. I think she's been poisoned.'

'It's him, that oul' fella next door. Him and his shaggin' canaries. He did it.' He sent my mother up to the room for salt and water and tried to make the cat sick. I prayed as I had never prayed before for Woolley to get better. My father prized open her mouth and poured in the emetic which dribbled out at the sides. 'Will she get better? She won't die, sure she won't?' I sobbed.

'Stop crying,' my mother said. 'You'll make yourself sick. Stop it.' And when I didn't she added, 'It's a sin to cry over a cat. A cat hasn't got a soul. Stop it when I tell you.'

Woolley was brought upstairs and laid near the fire. Before I

66

went to bed she died. My father was wondering aloud what had happened to her. My mother replied that she knew well the cause of it. That specky-eyed bastard had given her a dose of something. And if she could prove it she'd be in there and up-end him and his canaries. Despite it being a sin I cried for Woolley for several days. Coming across a small ball she had played with, the side of the chair where she used to sharpen her claws. And every time I looked at the doll's pram I could see her dressed in the bonnet and coat with her paws like hands laying on the apron and forgot it was a sin to grieve for an animal.

The death of the cat and her suspicions that the neighbour was to blame distracted my mother from her preoccupation with whatever it was that had been tormenting her. However the change didn't last long and when once again the atmosphere became uneasy I began wetting the bed. A regime was imposed where my intake of liquid was restricted and I was lifted before my mother and father went to sleep. One night after I had been put back into bed I heard my father come in. I knew by his voice that he had been drinking.

'A nice hour of the night to come home. Where have you been?' asked my mother who was darning his drawers.

'That's for me to know and you to find out.'

It was a reply that in the past had goaded her to erupt. I burrowed down in the bed not wanting to witness a row. But when I could hear nothing I became inquisitive and peered over the covers. My father was sitting by the fire holding his head in his hands. My mother stared at him—knocked out of her stride by his unusual pose.

'I'm going away,' he said. 'To England.'

'Well I hope it keeps fine for you,' my mother replied, trying to lighten the mood.

'I'm serious. I'm giving my notice on Monday.'

My mother dropped her mending and stood up.

'Have you lost your mind? I thought you were only joking. What about your work? You've a constant job. And in any case I don't want to go to England. And even if you got work over the other side you couldn't keep two homes going.'

'Listen,' he said, 'sit down, I've got something to tell you.'

'I'm all right where I am.'

'You're not making things easy.'

'Making things easy?' my mother said, her voice rising.

'You're deliberately making it difficult,' my father's voice too was loud. And then all of a sudden when my mother spoke it was in a tone she used to humour him when he was what she called 'half-cut'. So I thought he must be half-cut and likely to be the one to raise the row.

'I'll put the kettle on. I'll wet a sup of tea, you must be jaded. You won't be able to get up in the morning.' She began ladling water into the kettle from the enamel bucket, then lit the gas and put on the kettle.

My father continued talking. 'I want you to know about this. There's a girl.' My mother highered the gas. 'I never meant it to go so far. It was nothing.' Still my mother didn't say anything. She was putting cups on the table.

'We stopped seeing each other. But it was no use. So I'm going away.'

My mother leant over the table awkwardly so she wasn't face to face with him. When she spoke her voice was no longer conciliatory. 'I want to know nothing about it. Don't scald my heart by trying to ease your conscience.'

The kettle was boiling, steam gushing from the spout, the lid rattling. She lifted it, held it in her hand close to my father.

'Please God,' I prayed, 'don't let her throw it over him,' then shut my eyes.

Then I heard the water being poured into the teapot and my mother talking again.

'Don't come in here telling me about your fancy woman. I'm your wife, the mother of your three children.'

My father waved a hand in front of his face. 'I'm sorry. I'm sorry about everything. But I'm going. You won't be left short —I'll send your money regularly.' He was swaying in the chair, his head nodding forward.

'Oh Jesus!' my mother said and her voice sounded hoarse and choked. 'Why did you say anything? Why did you have to tell me? Why didn't you leave me alone? I had my suspicions but I didn't really want to know.'

My father's eyes were closed. He spoke without opening them. 'You'll be all right. I'll make sure of that. You won't go short.'

'Don't go. We can forget about it. Put it behind us. Don't

go, please.' I wished my mother would stop talking, would stop pulling at him, shaking him. 'Answer me,' she kept saying. 'You don't have to go. We can forget about it. Say something.'

He opened his eyes and looked up at her. He yawned and closed them again. 'Don't fall asleep, tell me you won't go. Only tell me that.'

'Saturday, a week Saturday. We're going a week Saturday.' And then he began snoring. I watched my mother, waiting for her to do something, to start screaming. She turned her head and looked towards the bed. I quickly closed my eyes and waited for a while before reopening them slightly. She had the corner of her pinnie up to her eyes wiping them and I knew she was crying and was very frightened for I had only seen her cry when someone died. I wanted to get out of bed and go to her and put my arms around her and say, 'Don't cry, I love you.' But I didn't really and anyway wasn't sure of how she would react. 'You bloody little knat,*' she might say, 'lying there letting on to be asleep and listening to everything that was going on.' You never knew what she might do. So I lay, and through half-closed eyes watched her as she went about the room tidying it, putting out clothes ready for the morning, hanging them over the fireguard to keep them warm. Sweeping the floor to discourage the mice. Now and then lifting her pinnie to her eyes and, before she undressed, loosening my father's tie and taking the front stud from his collar.

When I woke the next morning my father was gone. That wasn't unusual—often he left early to meet a body coming in on the boat. The bed was warm and comfortable. I was tired after the late night and didn't want to stir. Then suddenly I remembered his threat to go to England. Saturday he had said. Maybe he had gone sooner. Terrified that he had I sat up. 'Mammy, Mammy, where's Daddy gone?'

'To work—meeting the boat. Why?'

I mustn't let on I had heard the row. 'I only wondered.'

'Well stop wondering and get up. I'm taking you off school today. You're coming with me on an errand. Get up now.'

I was delighted at the prospect of no school. Quickly I got out of bed asking, 'To the market to buy something?'

---

* Pronounced kanat.

'To buy nothing.' Her preoccupied face and voice of the previous days were gone. This was her manner for doing battle with those who discommoded her. Rude civil servants, bumptious doctors, pompous priests or nuns and teachers who overstepped their role *in loco parentis.*

She gave me her lovely porridge—the consistency smooth and not too thick, swimming in milk. And afterwards bread crisply fried in beef dripping from the Sunday roast, browned in places with the delicious jelly. While I ate she talked to me, asking me questions, drawing me out.

'Did you ever go anywhere on a Sunday besides the Gallery, Museum, Botanical Gardens, Zoo or the relations?'

'No, only them.'

'You're sure—no where else at all?'

'Sometimes the Green.'

'Ah,' she said, 'I knew it. All the Sundays when the dinner was kept waiting. Who did you meet in the Green?'

'Nobody.'

'You must have met somebody.'

'I fell on the bridge and a woman gave me sweets.'

'Yes, go on.'

'She said I was very brave. She was from America, Daddy said.'

'Did you ever see her again?'

'I used to look for her but she never came back.'

Her lips were pursed and her fingers drummed on the table and her eyes held mine, staring so that I thought they could see inside my head. Searching and probing so that when I grew up I always found it difficult to tell her a lie.

'And no one else ever spoke to you or your daddy or gave you anything?'

'Only the girl in the sweet shop, Kathleen.'

'What sweet shop?'

She leant towards me, caught and pressed my hand.

'You're a good girl and you have a grand memory. What sweet shop, love?'

'Facing the stables. Where Daddy buys his cigarettes. She gave me lots of sweets and Half-Time-Jimmy and Daddy said if I told you you'd fight because it would spoil my dinner. She had a beret and her hair was in a fringe like mine. Only I got fed up waiting because they were always talking and laughing.'

'So that's her. Kathleen. Hurry now and finish your tea while I get the other two up and someone to mind them. Then I'm hotfoot down there. I'll soon put a stop to her gallop. The dirty little man mad bitch.'

We walked to Denzille Street. There was a pork shop near the tobacconist. We went in. There was a big fat woman shaking a metal cannister over a tray of pork chops, seasoning them.

'Yes ma'am,' she said.

My mother leant over the counter.

'I don't want to delay you, but I'm looking for someone who lives in the vicinity. A young wan with dark hair and she wears a beret.' Then she leant over the counter and whispered something to the woman.

'May God comfort you,' the fat woman said. 'I know her well and your husband too. A lovely looking man. She's a bold bitch, I've seen her swinging out of his arm, laughing up in his face. She works up in the Government Buildings. A right little whipster—a country wan. Her aunt's a decent woman.' She raised the counter flap. 'Come out to the door and I'll show you the shop.'

'God bless you,' my mother said.

'Ah, not at all, sure don't I know your predicament. There's plenty of young wans throwing theirselves at the men. Haven't I had the same trouble myself. A lot of forward little bitches.'

She came to the door and pointed out the sweet shop. 'Take my advice and go and see her aunt. Tell her everything—she'll soon put a stop to it. That's it there four doors along.'

As we reached the shop a hearse was coming out of the undertaker's yard, driven by a man neither my mother nor father liked. He spotted us and called 'hello' to my mother. After replying she said to me, 'wasn't I unfortunate meeting him above anyone. He's bound to tell your father.' Before going into the shop she looked in the window and touched her hair and moved her hat slightly. She always looked in mirrors and shop windows to see how she looked.

'A grand day,' the woman in the shop said, 'Can I get you anything?'

'Two penny-bars of Fry's chocolate and four Honey Bee bars, please.'

'That'll be fourpence. Isn't she a great girl,' she said smiling at me. The woman passed over the sweets and my mother gave her the money, then began to converse in the low voice she had used in the pork shop.

'God between us and all harm, ma'am, that's a terrible accusation to make. I think you're making a mistake.'

'There's no mistake. I don't think for a minute you've anything to do with it. I can tell by your face you're a God-fearing woman like myself. But the child knows her. She's been here time and time again.'

'I've never seen her before in my life. You have me at a disadvantage—I don't even know your name.'

'She comes of a Sunday, she knows her name and the woman in the pork shop has seen your niece with my husband, he works across the road.' She told the woman her name.

A man came into the shop for five Woodbines. The woman served him and when he was gone said, 'You'd better come inside—it's nearly dinnertime anyway. I'll close up.' She opened a section of the counter and a door into a little living-room. 'Go in there and sit down. I won't be a minute.'

We went in and sat down. My mother told me to stop fidgeting and not to get up or reach to touch anything. The woman came back. The table was laid with two plates of cold ham and pickles, bread and butter and a bottle of Lucknow sauce, two cups and saucers and a packet of fig roll biscuits.

The woman poked the fire and with her back to my mother spoke.

'I was a bit hasty ma'am. It was a terrible shock to hear such an accusation made against my niece. I know your husband only I didn't know he was anybody's husband. And of a Sunday I do go out for the day and Kathleen minds the shop.'

'I know how you feel,' said my mother. 'I know you'd never be a party to anything like that.'

'Indeed I would not.' The woman turned from the fire. 'I don't know what to say. She's like my own child. My sister's daughter, from Wicklow. When she got into the civil service she came to lodge with me. I've never had a minute's trouble with her. A good girl who minds her duties. Of course she's young and when she got taken up with ... well you know who I mean, I thought he was a bit too old for her—she's only a child not twenty till next month. But he seemed nice enough. Very respectful and I had to admit very handsome. So in the long run I raised no objection. Though from time to time I wondered how a fella like him had remained single so long. But I'll tell you one thing, now that I know the truth she's out of here—and her job. I'm down to the Government Buildings before the day is out. They won't condone carryings on. I'll tell them she's carrying on with a married man and unless there's an end to it I'll bring the priest on her. It's almost as if she knew you were coming—I've never known her to be so late for her lunch.'

The woman looked at the clock and I stood up and began to wander round the room. My mother ordered me back to her side saying to the woman if Kathleen saw me she'd know there was something up and maybe not come in at all. I came away from the glass-panelled door and sat down again.

Not long afterwards there was the sound of footsteps and the woman put her fingers to her lips. Kathleen came into the room. She had on her beret and I thought how nice she looked. She smiled at me and then looked from her aunt to my mother. My mother cleared her throat. She started to say something but the woman interrupted her. 'Do you know who this is?' she asked. Kathleen looked from me to my mother. 'I know the child,' she said. 'Then you knew he was a married man God forgive you,' my mother said.

'I tried to give him up. I did for a long time.'

'You're the cause of breaking up my home.'

'I'm not the one who is married.'

'Don't you talk to a decent respectable woman like that,' her aunt said.

'I could give you your character—but wouldn't pollute my lips to do so. But let me tell you this if you go to England with him you nor him will ever have an hour's luck. The curse of God will go with you.'

My mother's ankles were crossed and she held one hand in the other.

'England! Who said anything about England?' Kathleen asked and took off her beret. 'I don't know what you're talking about.'

'He told me himself. The two of you are going away next week.'

'That's all lies. There was never any mention of England.'

My mother got up and started walking towards Kathleen. 'Are you calling me a liar?' Her voice was angry.

'I don't think that's what she meant ma'am,' Kathleen's aunt said. 'And I think you'd be better leaving her to me. I'll see to it that you'll have no more trouble. In the name of God you'd be advised to go home now. If the circumstances were different I'd have offered you a pick.'

'So long as I have an assurance from her,' my mother said, collecting her bag and gloves.

Kathleen stood twirling the beret in her fingers but said nothing. 'Say something. Tell the woman you're ashamed of yourself—that you'll have nothing more to do with her husband.'

'It was never serious with me, only a bit of codding. There was nothing in it, nothing at all.' She began to cry. 'I never meant to cause trouble. We got into talk on Sundays when he came to buy his cigarettes. He's nice looking. We used to trick about. It just went on from there. I'm sorry.' She ran from the room.

Her aunt said, 'You'll hear no more about it ma'am. She's telling the truth and is sorry. I know her. But to make doubly sure I'll hold the threat of her losing her job and the priest over her.'

My mother said that God would reward her and that it was a pity there weren't more like her about. And she thanked her for being so civil.

My Aunt Maggie who had minded the children brought them back in the afternoon and was eager to hear if my mother had met Kathleen and if so how had the encounter gone. 'I met her all right. A brazen hussy. She stood her ground until the last minute. I felt like swinging out of her. A little bit of a thing. Young. All powder and paint like a doll. I wanted to get my hands on her. And would have done only her aunt was a decent respectable woman taking my side. I couldn't rise a scene in her home. The Kathleen wan said there was no foundation to the England thing. None whatsoever. I believed her.'

'D'ye want to know what I think,' asked my aunt Maggie and went on to tell her. 'He was getting in too deep. He wanted you to put a stop to it. At least he did last night but that might

74

have been the drink talking.'

'Well whether it was or not I've put a stop to it. The little bitch. Man mad—it was written all over her face.'

They talked for a while longer then my aunt had to go home but promised that later on she'd come back, listen at the door, and if my father was in she would go away, if he wasn't she'd come in.

Teatime came and no sign of my father. 'Keep a lookout for him,' my mother told me. It was getting dark. I watched through the window. The lamplighter came with his pole and a pool of yellowish light fell on the pavement. Later I knew children would come to make a swing. One climbing the lampost holding an orangebox rope in her teeth, then looping it round the standard, sliding down and pulling on the rope to make it taut. Afterwards they would take turns sitting in the fold of the rope to swing round and round the post. Their flight taking them out into the road where my mother forecast that one of them would be met by a lorry or a bus and have their brains dashed out.

The room grew dark and she lit the gas. Bringing a lighted spill from the fire and gently touching it to the fragile gas mantle. With a hiss a blue flame appeared at its base, its many tongues licking up the mantle's sides, and light flooded the room.

'You can come away from the window now,' she said and began making the tea. Talking aloud to herself as she did so. 'I wonder if he knows. He would if he'd run into that oul' bastard Mickey. Delighted he'd have been to give him the bang of seeing me outside the shop. And him knowing well what I was about.'

After tea the baby and my brother were put to bed. I'd be next.

I was in bed letting on to be asleep when my aunt came back. They sat by the fire and talked in whispers loud enough for me to hear.

'I think you'd be advised to sleep in my place tonight.'

'Why?' asked my mother.

'You never know what sort of humour he'll be in.'

'He's not the humoursome sort, thank God,' replied my mother.

'There's always the first time. He won't be jumping for joy knowing you went down to a place opposite his work. For you can bet your life Mickey will have lost no time telling him his little game was up.'

'And so it is. I don't see what that has got to do with me going over to your place.'

'Do, do,' I said to myself. Going out in the dark would be an adventure and I'd sleep in the bed with my Aunt Maggie.

'Telling you last night in a fit of drunken remorse was one thing. Maybe he thought you'd find Kathleen. Maybe that's what he wanted. What he wouldn't have taken into consideration was you being seen. Shaggin' men are bastards. Neither Mickey nor one of the others would have looked crooked at him while he was carrying on. They admire each other for that sort of thing. But the wife going to do battle with his fancy woman in full view of his work—that's a different kettle of fish. That's showing him up. Making a laughing stock of him.'

'You're not suggesting I shouldn't have gone?'

'You know bloody well I'm not,' my aunt retorted.

'What are you getting at then?'

'Praying that he comes in face falling ready only for sleep.' Through half-closed eyes I saw the look of puzzlement on my mother's face as she asked again what her sister was trying to say.

'I'm worried about what he might do. I'm afraid for you. I know more about men than you. Don't forget I've planted two of the bastards.'

'They were that all right. A pair of bowsies. Always ready with their hands. Is that what you're suggesting about my fella? Well let me tell you this. Never in his life drunk or sober has he raised a finger to me or my children.'

'You were lucky. With the knife-like tongue of yours many a man would have killed you. You take everything the wrong way. Twist everything. I know you can't help it. It's your nature. And I know he isn't a violent man. All I'm asking is don't put him to the test tonight. Come over to my place. Leave him a note. Let on I've been taken bad. If he's stocious he'll collapse and sleep. And if he's half-cut he won't follow you. What harm is there in that? You've come before when I was sick. He won't be suspicious. You've nothing to lose.'

'Mind your own business. He's my husband and I know how to handle him. I'd like you to go now. Your third husband may be a baa lamb but you'd never know a sudden change might come over him with you being out of your own place so long.'

Putting her coat on my aunt said, 'I hope you know what you are doing. If you want me you know where I am.'

I fell asleep and woke with a terrible fright. My mother was screaming. My father standing over her, hitting her with his fists. The baby and my brother woke and the three of us were screaming. Sidling down in the bed, terrified, but still watching, I saw blood running down my mother's face, falling on her white nightie, staining it bright red. And I thought how small she looked in her bare feet with her hair hanging down her back in a long plait.

Someone knocked on the door and then I heard the voice of the woman who lived on the landing calling, 'For the love of God will you leave the woman alone.' And I heard her turn the handle. But the bolt must have been on. The knob rattled and she called again. 'If you don't open this door I'm going for the police.' My father backed off and my mother ran and undid the bolt. The neighbour came in. 'May God forgive you to do that to your wife,' she said. 'I wouldn't have believed it of you. Look at her poor face.' My father never looked in her or my mother's direction. 'Here,' the woman said, 'hold that up to your lip, it's in gores.' She handed my mother a towel, found her coat and shoes and helped her into them.

I was afraid to move, looking from my father to my mother. I knew she was hurt and felt sorry for her. But she must have done something terrible. My father never started rows, my father was never cranky. The neighbour lifted and wrapped the baby in a blanket. 'I'll take him as well,' my mother said indistinctly through the folds of the towel through which the blood was soaking, pointing to my brother.

I waited for a little while after they left before sitting up. My father came and sat on the side of the bed. He was crying. I'd never seen him cry before.

'Were you awake all the time?' he asked.

I nodded my head. 'Oh my God,' he said. 'I'm so sorry. I never meant anything like that to happen. To hurt her. For you to witness such a thing. Oh, God, I'm so sorry.'

He was drying his eyes and blowing his nose. Then he saw the blood on his hands. He spread them out. 'Blood,' he said.

'Oh Jesus, I must have really hurt her.'

'It's on the floor as well,' I said.

He looked. 'So it is. It's everywhere. You should never have witnessed anything like that.'

'I want to do a wee-wee, can I get up? Can I?' I asked again when he didn't seem to have heard what I had said.

'Yes, yes, no, wait. I'll have to wipe the floor first.'

I watched him clean the floor and wash his hands.

He made me cocoa and then I went to sleep. When I woke again it was morning. He was getting ready for work when my mother and her sister came in. 'I hope,' she said, 'you're proud of your handiwork. Seven broken ribs and six stitches in her lip.' He wouldn't look at either her or my mother. He took his coat and began brushing it while my aunt continued to berate him. And I thought how brave he was to be brushing his coat and ignoring all the abuse he was getting.

After he went my aunt said, 'If you don't put in for a separation after this don't come knocking on my door again in the middle of the night.' She raked the fire and got it going. 'Sit down,' she told my mother, 'You look ready to collapse.' She made breakfast and helped me get ready for school and talked to my mother at the same time. 'Not a judge in the land will refuse the separation when he hears about his fancy woman and sees the state of you. I'll give you all the assistance you need. I'll see you don't starve.'

My mother's mouth was swollen to twice its size. She sat staring into the fire and for once let her sister talk without interrupting her.

EIGHT

For several days my father didn't come home. My aunt and the neighbours came in to help with the housework, lifting the pram up and down the stairs and fetching the buckets of water. If my mother sneezed she cried out with the pain in her ribs and she could only eat slops for her mouth was still swollen.

I wondered if my father would ever come back, wanting to talk to my mother about it but not daring. Then one evening I heard the familiar footsteps on the stairs. I began to go towards the door but my mother forbade me. He brought sweets, a bag of marbles for my brother and for the baby a pink celluloid rattle. He kissed me and then my brother, who pulled away from him. I followed him about the room.

'I got the summons,' he said. My mother didn't say anything.

'I'm sorry. I didn't mean to hurt you—I was drunk.'

My mother remained silent. He put the kettle on the gas and cut bread and cheese.

'Will you have anything to eat?' he asked.

'No,' my mother said.

'I said I'm sorry. What more do you want?'

'Nothing. This time next week you'll be gone from here thank God. You'll never come in again to terrify me and your innocent children.'

'If you're going to start I'm leaving.' He put down the half-eaten sandwich. 'I came with the best intentions. I thought we could talk—make things up. But have it your way.'

I started to cry when he left. Crying that I'd never see him again—that he was gone forever. I said I didn't want him to go, that I loved him.

'And he loves you too and all of you. He's a good father,' was all she said about him to us. All she was ever to say about him; never trying to curry favour in our eyes, never trying to blacken him.

My mother borrowed a coat from her sister and retrimmed a hat for her court appearance.

'It's a pity your lip has gone down,' my aunt said to her on the day before the hearing while my mother was trying on the clothes.

'Why?' asked my mother turning from the mirror.

'What d'you mean, why? Wouldn't it have said more for you than any amount of words?'

'Yes, and made me an eye-sore,' my mother retorted, turning back to the glass. She adjusted the brim of the hat, saying 'I think it looks better tilted to the side.'

'It's looking for a separation you are, not going to a party!'

'Wherever I'm going I like to look my best.' My mother took off the coat, hung it up and carefully placed the hat in a large brown paper bag which served as her hatbox. Putting it in the sideboard she warned me not to touch near it.

'Of course it'll go in his favour that he's never kept you short.'

'Never in his life,' replied my mother. 'Not even now when he's living out of the house. My wages were sent up on Saturday and with an extra five shillings.'

'The way you say that I can see you're half way to forgiving him already,' my aunt said as she prepared to go home.

'Indeed faith I am not. Wouldn't I be a fool to be palmed over that easy?'

The next morning I watched my mother getting ready to go to court. She brushed her hair for a long time before arranging it in two coils on either side of her head. She looked at herself sideways on in the mirror and talked to herself saying she wished she had a new stays. The bones in this one were no good. Smoothing her hands over her stomach she told herself she looked like a sack tied up in the middle. But that she'd have to do and thank God the coat was semi-fitting. Then she couldn't find her hatpin and blamed me for moving it. 'I put it there—on the corner of the table. You must have disturbed it. You're always meddling with things. Now what'll I do? Your aunt'll be here in a minute and me not ready.'

She looked everywhere, under the table, on the mantlepiece, in other hats, scolding and blaming me all the time. Until suddenly she remembered where the pin was. 'In your granny's jewellery box. Hand it to me.' The sides of the box were made of heavy glass through which I could see the ornate imitation-pearl-encrusted hatpin lying on the faded pale blue padded velvet bottom beside two locks of hair, one black and lustrous and one lank and yellow white. When my mother was good humoured she would tell me that the dark lock had been snipped from my grandmother's hair six weeks before she got cancer and the other when she died. 'Seventy she was. She lived to see you and draw her pension. Seventy years of age and not a grey hair.' I handed her the box and she secured the hat.

I had only a vague understanding of what was happening but knew that my father might never come home and was broken-hearted imagining never seeing him again. Wondering where he would sleep and who would cook his dinner.

During the morning of the court hearing I was looked after by a neighbour who lived across the road. A kind gentle woman who had a large family. Some of her daughters were close to me in age and we played well together in the large overgrown garden. In a corner of the garden, behind a makeshift fence, one of the tenant's kept a pig who squealed, grunted and rooted amongst his straw and the peelings and stale bread on which he was fed. On the morning my mother went to court the big girls bought pennyworths of dolly clothes, scraps of stuff from the local dressmaker with which to make numerous ensembles for our dolls. Being one of the youngest I wasn't allowed to cut out but was permitted to tack the pieces of art-silk, serge, wool and taffeta. Between dressmaking and tormenting the pig I forgot all about what might happen if the separation order was granted.

At dinner time I was petted by the family and encouraged to eat my stew made from lap of mutton—a meal my mother never cooked because she said it was too greasy. I forced myself to swallow the strips of lean sandwiched between the layers of mutton-fat and, when she wasn't looking at me, I studied the woman's face and wondered about the terrible secret which I had heard my mother and her sister hint at. 'Poor Kate,' they would say, 'Isn't it a terrible burden to carry a secret like that.'

After dinner I kept going in and out to the hall door

watching for my mother to come home. When she and my aunt did come into sight they were talking animatedly to each other. I called out. My mother shouted back that I was not to run across the road until she told me I could. Safely over, I followed them up the stairs and into the room where once inside the door my aunt said, 'I can't get over it—the bloody oul' shite refusing the order.'

'Keep your voice down,' my mother said. 'I don't want her next door to know my business.'

'She'll know it soon enough when he comes home, or the next time he splits your lip.'

'He'll never lay a finger on me again. The judge bound him over to keep the peace for two years.'

'Bound him up and thrown him in the Liffey—that's what he should have done. What in the name of Christ is the matter with men like him? Didn't he have all the evidence? What does a husband have to do—kill his wife before a judge sees the light of day?'

'There's more to it than that,' my mother said, removing her hatpin and telling me to put it in the jewellery box, then removing her hat and placing it in its paper box.

'When I think of it my blood ...'

'I think you've said enough,' my mother said as she took off my aunt's coat, handed it to her and exaggeratedly thanked her for the loan of it.

'So you're on your high horse,' her sister said. 'I might have known it—you never wanted a separation in the first place.'

'It wasn't me that refused it. You heard what he said when the judge asked him if he wanted one. "No your Lordship," he said. "I love my wife. I don't want to part from her. I love my children." You heard him—you were there.'

'Oh Jesus give me patience. You were sucked in by that. After all he's done on you—beating and his fancy woman and you fell for that.'

'Now you listen to me. I'm fed up with you telling me what to do. Making cutting remarks about my husband. I love him. No matter what he does nothing will ever alter that. I love him. And don't think because I was beholden to you for the lend of a coat you can browbeat me into thinking otherwise. Thank you for coming with me but if it's all the same I think you should go home now.'

Now my mother was fighting with my aunt and she might go away like my father and never come back. I thought I hated her. Then she said to me, 'Kiss your aunt goodbye and then I want you to go for a message—your father will be home in a minute and I've nothing for his tea.'

I was so happy that I ran all the way to the pork shop and didn't pick the meat.

The following months were the happiest I ever remembered. My father didn't go out in the evenings. Because of this my mother's wages were increased. She was good humoured all the time; singing when she washed the clothes and cleaned the place. Smiling a lot, listening when I came home from school with something to tell her, and best of all she had started reading me *The Old Curiosity Shop*. Together we cried when 'Little Nell' died and my father comforted me and told me it was only a story.

Then we got a wireless—one of the first families in the street to have one. 'Of course,' my mother told her sister proudly, 'my fella's always been mad about music.'

'Isn't everyone in Dublin,' my aunt countered. 'There's few families that haven't sat in the gods and listened to the best artists in the world. You only have to hear the singing of a Saturday night after the pubs shut. None of your oul' come-all-yes. You can hear anything from the *Bohemian Girl* to *Cavalleria Rusticana*.'

My father took my mother to the theatre and the cinema—one of the girls whose mother had a terrible secret minded us. Sometimes they brought back fish and chip suppers which I shared. When the weather got fine we took a tram out to Rathfarnham and brought a picnic. And one day I heard my mother tell her sister that thanks be to God she had never been so comfortable in her life and that if only she could get a house with a shut hall door she'd be on the pig's back.

We heard new songs on the wireless and my father bought song books from which we learned the words. Neighbours were invited to come and listen and advised to get a wireless—there was nothing like them, my father said—a great invention to keep you in touch with the world. Our lovely happy life continued. In fine weather we went for picnics. Taking a tram or a bus out of the city. To places in the mountains, in the pine forest, to a lake that was the city's reservoir. There were trees and streams to fish, ponds across which dragonflies skimmed, fairy-like creatures with gauzy wings hovering, swooping, vanishing and reappearing again as if from nowhere. Placid cows with swollen udders gazed at us from large gentle eyes, cows so dissimiliar to those I had only ever seen running, being beaten and hastened through the narrow streets towards their death.

Under a tree or near a grassy hillock my mother spread the tablecloth and unpacked the picnic while my father collected twigs for the fire. She instructed him to plug the nose of the kettle with a wad of newspaper to prevent the tea being smoky. The fire was a Godsend, my mother said. As well as boiling the water it kept the midges away. The sandwiches, pies, cakes and biscuits were gorged. My mother commenting that nothing gave you an appetite like fresh air. The baby toddled about, pulled handfuls of grass which when my mother looked away for a moment she tried to eat. My brother and my father went exploring and brought back forks of branches suitable for making a sling. He told us the names of different trees, oaks and silver birches, sweet and horse chestnuts, the hornbeam from which he said butchers' blocks were made and the elms whose wood was used for coffins. In England, he said, when he was a little boy they went bird nesting. Once a friend of his put his hand in a nest and was bitten by an adder. But it couldn't happen in Ireland—there were no snakes and in any case we should never rob nests. With morbid curiosity I wanted to know what happened to the boy. Had he died? 'No,' my father said, 'a man in the woods gave him first-aid and then he went to the hospital.'

'What's first-aid?' I asked.

'Don't ask so many questions, you're a very curious child,' my mother told me. My father showed us how to make whistles from dandelion stalks. Snapping off the bright yellow heads you blew down the stem and it whistled. Milk leaked from the injured flesh and tasted bitter on my lips. 'You can feel the benefit of a day in the country,' my mother would say as we travelled the few miles home. 'One day maybe we'll have a real holiday—rent a place in Rush. But still and all I'd rather have somewhere on the southside. Bray's nice, or Killiney.'

'Anywhere,' my father agreed. I sat lost in thought imagining a real holiday. No one I knew ever went on holidays. But there were pictures in story-books of people on holidays at the seaside.

They went by train carrying attaché cases. And carried buckets and spades, fishing nets on long cane handles and enormous, coloured beach balls. I'd have new canvas shoes with a strap and button, proper girls' summer shoes and new dresses, shantung with a cape collar, sleeveless, trimmed with bright braid. All day we would play on the beach, I might learn how to swim. And in the rock pools would be creatures, crabs, shrimps and anemones which I would catch in my net. It would be wonderful—like Christmas in the summer.

* * *

I was the best reader in the class and enjoyed being asked to read aloud. Reading, I was careful to pronounce my words correctly, pause and count one at a comma and two at a full stop. I gave my performance conscious that I had a captive audience, if only because the nun would slap or send out of the room anyone who broke the silence. Afterwards she would congratulate me and tell the class that that was how English should be spoken. 'None of your *dis* and *dat*. No dropping the gs at the end of a word ending in -*ing*.' On the blackboard she chalked this and that. 'Now let me hear how you pronounce them.'

'This and that,' said the class.

'And again.'

'This and that, Sister.'

'Well remember it now. And when you are talking we don't want to hear anything about *Mr and Mrs Do Be* and all the little *Does Bes*.' Again the class gave its assent.

Reading and reciting, sounding my *gs* and omitting the *Do Bes* family, earned me praise from my English teacher but sometimes after a lesson if we went out to play certain of the children took their revenge by chanting 'Katy the shaper, Curled her hair with paper, The shaper slipped and cut her lip, Katy the shaper.' But the next day after the singing or sewing lesson I would be back in favour with them. At singing and sewing I was no good.

'But you must be able to sing—you have a good speaking voice,' Sister Theresa said. 'Come out here and sing the scales.' It was the only lesson during which I was wilfully disobedient, refusing to sing even though it meant being slapped. 'Why? Answer me that or you'll be slapped again.'

'I can't sing, Sister.'

'There's no such a word as can't.'

My mother told me I couldn't sing. Usually she would continue the song I had begun, singing at the top of her voice, able to reach the highest note or lower her voice. Though I doubted many other things she told me, I believed she was right—I'd never make a singer. Alone in the room after her rebuff I felt stupid and foolish—to sing the scale in front of thirty girls who would surely, despite the nun's vigilance, titter, I would die of shame or, worse, break down and cry.

The needlework teacher did no coaxing. Showed no surprise that the two-inch long, one-inch wide piece of pink or green lawn was cobbled instead of flat-hemmed or French-seamed; that my buttonhole on a similar sized piece of stuff was alternately frayed or the thread gathered in a tangle of knots, and often the coloured lawn stained with blood from my pricked finger. 'You lazy, worthless girl,' and a bang of the ruler across the knuckles was all the attention I was worth or she had time for.

But there were other days when I came into my own— English composition, Religious Knowledge or any subject where my jackdaw memory could shine. Sums and Irish I put far from my mind.

A dancing teacher came once a week and those who paid extra had lessons. Soon, my mother promised, I could join the class. The lessons were held after school and in fine weather in the playground. I stopped by the railings and watched the girls learn how to dance a reel. 'One, two, three, four, five, six, seven, back one, two, three' called the teacher, clapping her hands in time to the piano.

'When can I go, Mammy, say when, please,' I'd plead when I came in from school.

'Next week, or the week after. I'll get you a pair of pumps. Irish dancing gives you a lovely carriage. Next week definitely.' Next week definitely, like one day we'll go to the seaside, was, I discovered, a promise made to be broken. From time to time I renewed my efforts at persuasion. Then gave up, until I discovered that fancy dancing was being taught as well as Irish. The little dancers talked excitedly about tap-shoes, end of term concerts, tambourines, gypsy costumes, going on the stage. You might even, one day, be a chorus girl. All of this I related to my mother, begging and pleading to be allowed to join the dancing class.

'Fancy dancing! Tap dancing! Chorus girl! And finish up showing your arse on the stage. You're going to no dancing classes and don't let me hear you mention it again,' was her reply.

I gave up and concentrated on collecting cigarette cards. Studying the beautiful pictures of wildflowers and fresh-water fish and becoming a good marble player. One day while I was playing, the girl, whose leadener I was about to win, said, 'Your mother's having a baby.'

'I know,' I lied.

'And do you know what will happen her—her belly will get big.' She stretched her arms wide.

'I know,' I repeated as I pocketed her large ballbearing.

'I'm not playing any more and my brother will kill me for losing his leadener. Can I have it back?'

'No, I won it.'

'And do you know what happens after she gets that big— she'll burst—that's how they come out, the babies—you know.'

'I'm going home,' I said, and on the way wondered if babies were inside their mothers' bellies.

Lately I had wondered about this a lot. Sometimes I thought they were. But you couldn't be sure. Some women with big bellies did have new babies, but others of the same size didn't. And men had big bellies too. If the babies were inside their mothers how did they get out? As to how they got in I had no idea—the nurse didn't bring them in her black bag. It was too small and they'd smother. Maybe the hospitals did sell them. Then where did the women who never went into hospital get them? Or the woman I had heard my mother tell her sister about who had a baby in a field? It was all lies, I was beginning to suspect. Like Daddy Christmas and Prince, maybe even the fairies. Though I didn't want to dismiss the fairies just yet. Fairies were magic and could grant you wishes. And there was a banshee. I often heard her wailing at night. 'Listen,' my mother would say, 'that's her, she's come to warn a family that someone is going to die. Thanks be to God she doesn't folly our family.' So if there were bad fairies there could be good fairies.

Nearing the house, my pocket heavy with chalk marbles and the big, smooth steel one, I imagined meeting a fairy. If I got up very early while the dew was still on the ground and went to the haggard, one might appear. She would be wearing a white dress, shimmering with tinsel and her gaudy wings like those of a dragon fly quivering in the breeze. Then she would raise her wand and grant me a wish. What would I ask for—I knew—the secret about babies. My mother's stomach didn't look any different. I watched her for a few days but she was still the same. That Hannah was a terrible liar.

Then one day my mother came from the market and after unpacking her shopping, held up a book and said, 'Do you see this? Well if ever I catch you going near it I'll cut the legs from under you. Do you understand?'

'Yes Mammy,' I replied, deciding that at the first opportunity I would root everywhere until I found the book I knew she would hide.

NINE

'**A**h, do you know who's dead?' my mother asked one night looking up from the death column in the *Herald* which was the first and sometimes the only thing she read in the evening paper.

'Who?' my father questioned.

'You wouldn't know him. Lord have mercy on his soul. Molly's husband—you wouldn't know her either.'

'Oh,' said my father returning to his book.

'I used to work with her. I remember them courting. God be with the days. Mind you he was no good—gave her a terrible life. The Lord have mercy on him.'

'Who's burying him?'

'Fanagans. In Glasnevin after nine mass in the morning.'

'You're not going?' my father asked concernedly.

'You wouldn't think it advisable?'

'Not in your condition and the weather so bad. Drop her a line.'

'I suppose you're right. I always think deaths go in threes—hear of one and you'll hear of two more before the year is out, don't you?'

My father was engrossed again in his book and made no reply.

My mother handed me the paper. 'Read 'Mutt and Jeff' and then get ready for bed.'

Then Hannah was right. She was having a baby. Her belly wasn't big but she had stitched a loop of elastic on the waist of her skirt to reach the button and when she wasn't wearing her pinnie I could see her slip where the skirt-placket gaped.

I lay in bed and thought again about babies and fairies and having a wish. Then I remembered the book. If I asked a fairy to make me invisible I could find that. Watch my mother reading it and afterwards hiding it and she'd never know I was watching her. Just before I fell asleep I remembered that tomorrow was Shrove Tuesday and we'd have pancakes. I loved pancakes.

The house smelled of frying batter and lemon juice. My mother and the woman who lived in the room on the landing were making pancakes. I had already sampled the trial one and was eagerly waiting for my father to come home when the rest would be eaten. As soon as I heard his whistle I raced down to the hall and met him. Coming up the stairs we stood to one side to let Lizzie, one of the children from the house, pass. She smiled at us and my father touched her wild curly hair and told her she was getting to be a big girl.

The pancakes were wafer thin, sugared and lemony. My mother stood by the stove pouring batter into the iron frying pan. As fast as she piled the plates as fast they were cleared. The wireless was playing, a man singing 'We'll Build a Garden in Granada'.

'Shh,' my mother said, 'what's that?'

'Nothing,' my father replied after listening. 'Are there any more?'

'For God's sake give me a minute,' my mother said good-humouredly. 'Listen there is something up. I can hear a commotion.'

She went to the window and looked out. 'Oh my God, there's been an accident. Someone knocked down.'

'Where? Let me see.' My father joined her and they both stared down into the street. Suddenly there was noise everywhere. The sound of heavy footsteps running up the stairs, a door being pounded and then the most awful terrifying scream.

'Oh sweet Jesus, it's someone from next door. One of the children. Oh may God comfort her. I'll have to go in. Please God don't let it be anything serious.'

My mother was going out of the room followed by my father. The pan was smoking. My father noticed it and turned off the gas. From next door came the sound of a lot of people crying. I looked out through the window and saw a bus pulled into the side of the road, a crowd of people and an ambulance slowing down.

My mother was crying when she came back.

'Lizzie was run over. Me and your Daddy are going with them to the Meath.' She was taking off her pinnie and putting on her coat and hat. 'Be a good girl and mind them until I come back.' She secured the fire-guard and strapped the baby, who seldom now used the pram, into it.

'If anything goes wrong knock for Kitty, but not unless you have to. She's in a terrible state about her little sister.'

From the window I watched Lizzie's parents and mine cross the road and walk in the direction of the hospital. It started to rain heavily and I wondered if my father, who was only wearing his jacket, would come back for his overcoat and hat. But they all kept on walking until they were out of sight. The ambulance was gone, but the bus and the crowd were still there. I came away from the window and for a little while I thought about Lizzie and remembered the day John-Joe was knocked down when he chased my red balloon. My brother was looking at a book and the baby amusing herself trying to undo her harness. The sight of the book in my brother's hand reminded me of the forbidden one and I desperately wanted to see it. Under the beds and in the press, in my mother's hat-bag, amongst the clothes in the cupboard I searched. Then my father's tool-box that had his shoemaking last, heel-ball, nails and lengths of hemp, but no book. Then I had an idea—it might be in the well of the pram.

The baby, delighted that she was being released, struggled to assist me, making the undoing of the fleece-lined leather straps, which were already swollen and misshapen, more difficult. I was in a hurry—my mother could come back any minute. I shouted at her. Her bottom lip curled and she looked at me reproachfully while her eyes filled with tears. I kissed her and loved her and hushed her. Out of the pram she sat contentedly on the floor munching a piece of pancake while I took out the bedding and lifted up the little cover and there in the well amongst cake and bread crumbs was a package wrapped in a piece of oilskin. I felt it—it was a book. I longed to undo it—have a glimpse of the book. But dared not for if my parents came in I'd be in double trouble. My mother's reaction I could bear, being used to the slaps, threats and scolding. My father showed his disapproval in a more effective way, nothing dramatic—a look, a quietly spoken word. 'Taking the baby out of the pram is dangerous. Don't you know that?' Always I wanted to please him—to be the best—the cleverest—the most loving. Never to fail in his estimation of me. So quickly I replaced the book and rearranged the pram. When my parents returned everything was as it should be.

'Poor little Lizzie died ten minutes after we arrived. Her mother and father are distracted with grief. It's a terrible thing to lose a child. Amn't I always telling you about the traffic.'

Gathering me and my brother into her arms my mother said, 'Won't you be very careful on the road. Poor little Lizzie. May God comfort them next door and spare you to me.'

'They're Lizzie's boots,' I said, wriggling from her embrace and pointing to the short, shabby brown button-boots my father had put near the hearth. Many times I had envied Lizzie the boots which sometimes she wore with buff-coloured gaiters that a well-off relation had given to her, complete with a button-hook for fastening the long rows of buttons.

'There's still a lot of wear in them. I'll give the socks a lather and your Daddy will polish the boots then after the funeral I'll let her mother have them back. They'll give one of the others a turn.'

On the day of the funeral I got my opportunity to see the book. One of the girls whose mother had a terrible secret was minding us. The baby was asleep on the bed and the girl stretched out beside her reading *Red Letter*. I knew she didn't care what we did so long as her reading wasn't interrupted.

I could only read one word of the title, *Midwives*, but inside there were pictures on almost every page, black and white. Peculiar drawings that made no sense to me. I couldn't read the words either except for the very simple ones. But I kept turning the pages until I came to the babies. Difficult at first to identify as babies, upside down, naked and with huge heads curled inside something. Turning more pages I saw the babies again—this time unmistakably inside their mothers—women with no clothes on either. I studied the drawings going back to the previous pages, looking at squiggly things that made no sense then back to the babies inside their mothers. And though I went over every page to the end of the book all I got for my trouble was the fact that babies were in women's bellies but was left as much in the dark as to how they got out. Maybe Hannah was right and they did burst.

In the weeks after Lizzie's death on several occasions my mother reminded my father that she had said 'hear of one death and you'll hear of another two'. And one evening added 'God between us and all harm I wonder who'll be next?'

'As long as we get the funeral I don't care,' my father replied.

'That's an awful thing to say.'

'It's what feeds us,' my father reminded her.

'I suppose you're right,' my mother agreed, 'but all the same it sounds callous put like that.'

TEN

I wouldn't give Hannah the satisfaction of knowing she was right about babies so decided to describe what I had seen in the book to another girl. She was a quiet, gentle girl who although she wore red ribbons in her hair and brought flowers for the altar had never been over the press.* Her name was Rosaleen and I felt sorry for her because she had a hare-lip.

'If I tell you a secret say "Cross my heart and hope to die" that you'll never let on.'

She crossed her heart and hoped to die, but didn't seem very surprised when I described what I'd seen in my mother's book.

'I bet you never knew that,' I whispered when the nun again turned her back on the class.

'No,' she said, 'never.'

'Well then?' I asked.

'Well then what?' she said.

I couldn't think of a reply but decided that I'd tell her no more secrets.

The book and the babies went out of my mind, for the skipping season had started. From a vegetable shop the big girls had bought a straw rope that came round the orange boxes. And after school in a street where no traffic came a girl stood on either side of the road turning the long rope. Through it we skipped, one after the other, while everyone chanted 'Chase, chase, chase the fox,' on and on until, when a skipper tangled with the rope, it became her turn at the rope's end. There were three glorious afternoons of skipping, other chanting songs were

---

* Been the child in charge of dispensing copybooks, etc. from the press in the classroom.

93

sung and more complicated skipping feats performed. One where you skipped faster and faster and the turners increased their pace of turning and the onlookers called 'Salt, Vinegar, Pepper, Pepper, Pepper' and you skipped and skipped, until, exhausted, you stumbled and tangled your feet in the rope and the chant changed to 'You're out, You're out.'

Then home for tea, something special that my mother had baked, a story before bed and the promise of a second-hand scooter my mother had seen on her market expeditions. I was the happiest girl in the world until the fourth morning after telling Rosaleen my secret when I was summoned to Mother Bonaventure's office. Immediately I knew something out of the ordinary had happened. Parents went to the office to complain or look for charity; objecting to the caning of a child, asking for free shoes or school books. Very bold girls who cursed were called to the office, and occasionally one who had raised a hand to a nun. I was never that bold so I was curious rather than fearful.

I knocked on the door and waited for permission to enter. Mother Bonaventure sat behind her desk, her plump pale face not creased by the usual smile. I felt the first flutter of fear. She beckoned me to her. I hesitated short of the desk and she said, 'Come right up child, right up to the desk', and still she didn't smile. I loved this nun. I worked harder for her than anyone else. Writing and rewriting my compositions so that I won her praise, so that she smiled at me and sometimes touched my head in passing. I knew how many black-headed pins she wore in her veil. Could, had I chosen, have imitated how she moved, told what her hands and nails were like, described how, in the oratory, when mass was being celebrated and the long black robe worn pinned up at the hem let loose, it followed her up the aisle like a bride's train. I knew and loved the sweet clean smell of her.

Now she regarded me with a severe disapproving look. I waited and waited for her to speak. 'Rosaleen's mother came to see me this morning,' she said. The bellies! The babies! That little sneak had told her mother. Oh my God! You weren't supposed to know about babies—they were like dirty things. Oh God please let me die. Make Mother Bonaventure stop looking at me like that. I felt faint the way I did after fasting before communion. Breaking out in a cold sweat—then roasting, my heart pounding.

'Where did you get the book?'

I couldn't talk, I was choking.

'Well—I'm waiting. Where did you get this book?'

'I ... It was ... I ...'

'Yes, go on.'

I started to cry, quietly at first then uncontrollably, sobs hiccuping through me, feeling each one making me want to vomit. My mind raced in time with my heart. I'd be sick all over the desk. I'd wet myself. I'd die and then they'd all be sorry. My mother would find out and my father. Mother Bonaventure would never like me again. Shame and fear and at the same time an awareness that my plight—the wracking sobs, the tears streaming down my face—might arouse in her some pity, sympathy, even leniency.

'Drink this.' There was no hint of leniency in her tone as she handed me the tumbler. 'Blow your nose, wipe your eyes and stop crying.'

I searched for a hankie I knew I didn't have. 'Use this,' she commanded. It smelled of her. I could have held it to my face for ever, hiding my eyes from hers I blew my nose and wiped my eyes and felt sorry for what I had done and very sorry for myself.

'That's better. Come and sit down. Here.' She pointed to a chair near the desk. 'Ah,' she said, 'I'm disappointed in you.' I looked down at my feet and twisted the hankie into a ball. 'You were disobedient and deceitful. Why?'

'I only wanted to see what the book was like.'

'Look at me when you speak. Could you read this book and did you understand it?'

'Only the pictures.'

'Pictures of what?'

'Babies and women in their skin.'

'And what exactly did you tell Rosaleen?'

'That—about babies growing in their mammys' bel... stomachs.'

'Some books are not suitable for children. That's why your mother forbade you to read it. You are a very curious little girl. Curiosity can be a good thing if it is used properly. It is good to want to know about things—to ask questions and read about them. But until you are much older you have to be led in what you read by grown-ups. The nuns and your mother and father. Do you understand that? At the moment where babies grow should be no concern of yours. There are millions and millions of subjects far more interesting for a child of your age. Now listen carefully to what I am going to say. You know, because of your disobedience, that Our Lord lets babies grow inside their mothers. I doubt if any other child in the school knows that and I want you to promise me that you will not tell them. I want you to promise me that.'

'Oh yes Mother—I'll never tell anyone, never.'

'I am trusting you.' For the first time since I had entered the office there was the hint of a smile. 'I don't expect you to break your word.'

'Oh no Mother I wouldn't as true as God.'

'I won't tell your mother. But you must confess your sin of disobedience in confession. And in future if there's something you want to know talk to your parents or come to me. All right?'

Eagerly I promised all she asked.

'Your handkerchief,' I said.

'Keep it. Go now and bathe your eyes and then straight back to your classroom and remember our promises.'

I loved her more than ever and I would never again be disobedient or deceitful. And I never ever wanted to know anything else about babies. And I'd never tell Rosaleen another secret or feel sorry for her hare-lip. I went home the long way and dawdled looking at the shop windows. Outside the pawn hung three brass balls. Here there was nothing to buy for a penny or a ha'penny but plenty to see. The window was full of unredeemed pledges. Silver sports trophies, wedding rings, engagement rings with rubies and diamonds, razor and christening mugs, watches, ornaments and cases of medical students' equipment.

In the pork shop window, two fat pigs stood on their hind legs offering trays of plaster sausages and black puddings. Large joints of finely scored roast pork, crisply crackled, and with stuffing oozing out of them, made my mouth water. Through the window of the provision shop I watched the woman selling butter. Saw her clap with wooden clappers the great creamy mound into quarters, two-ounce and half-pound portions. The leather shop was dark and dusty. Beside squares of leather sold for boot mending there were hanks of wax thread, awls, assorted nails, sharp knives, brown and black heel-ball, and the little iron gadgets with which it was applied to the newly mended footware. One small shop sold coal by the stone and half-stone. It lay in a heap on the floor beside a big brass scales. The shop also sold paraffin oil, bundles of sticks, pot menders for holes in enamel basins, jugs and pots, and the beautiful gas mantles fragile as dandelion clocks. Then there was the hay shop with nothing only bales of hay in the window, thousands of hayseeds outside on the path and the lovely smell of hay. I stood looking into the window of the chemists where I went to buy cough bottles for my father. Admiring the tall beautiful jars, blue and green and red like the sapphires, rubies and emeralds that were in engagement rings. There were boat-shaped feeding-bottles with teats on either end and rolls of thermagene wadding, bundles of sugar-barley sticks, pots of Ponds Vanishing Cream, green and cream coloured tins of Zambuk ointment and big fluffy powder-puffs. And something I wanted and hoped I would get when I grew up—tiny flasks of Evening in Paris, Californian Poppy and Phulnana perfumes. Stopping by the door to look inside I saw the big weighing-scales and the small basket one for weighing babies, the cupboards lining the wall behind the counter with tiny drawers, each one labelled. Breathing in a big breath of the many lovely smells, I left and made my way home.

'Didn't I tell you to come straight home from school. I never knew such a disobedient child in all my life,' my mother said when I came in.

Two weeks later my mother miscarried. She had to stay in bed for a week and while she was laid up her sister and the neighbours came to do the washing, cook, and mind the baby. There was always someone there when I came in from school. After been given my tea they forgot about me and talked—I listened. Miscarriages were worse than births, they said. And they were nearly always boys. Boys were hard to carry. But it was God's will. Wasn't it better to lose a child then than give birth to an 'invicile'. You miscarried because the child you were carrying was flawed. Another woman countered that God's ways were sometimes hard to fathom. For hadn't He let poor Janey Morrissey carry three boys full term for them to come into the world with heads the size of footballs. She was contradicted. 'That was their father's fault, wasn't he riddled with the bad disease.' But they all agreed that death came in threes.

And to add more credence to the superstition my mother quoted the death of Lizzie, her friend's husband in the hospice and now her miscarriage. She told how on the night Lizzie was knocked down my father had gone with her mother and father to the hospital. How it was lashing out of the heavens and in the hurry he had gone in his bare head and without an overcoat, was soaked to the skin and had had a cold on his chest ever since.

Advice came from every side. Certain cough bottles worked miracles with chesty coughs. She should buy a roll of thermagene wadding and make a vest of it for him to wear next to his skin. Then when the weather got warm pick a pinch off every day, so he wouldn't feel the loss suddenly. By the end of May the last pick would be pulled and he'd be a new man.

One day the woman with the terrible secret was there. She had a lump in her breast and the women urged her to go and see about it. Offering to go with her. Telling her the name of a grand man who sat in the Adelaide on a Friday. You'd be hours waiting to see him but it was worth it. And say what you liked about the hospitals run by the Irish Sweepstakes not one could touch the Protestant hospitals. They were the best in the city of Dublin and no nun treating you like dirt or meeting you up in the face with the almoner's box when you didn't have the price of your bus-fare. After the woman went home, I heard the others say, 'Poor Kate, she's finished, her face's the colour of saffron.'

And another voice added, 'God help her and she still with her terrible secret.'

'What secret is that?' asked a newcomer to the group.

'Didn't she marry her first cousin without him or her knowing it. Two brothers' children. Him from the North and her from Dublin. Never laid eyes on each other before. Of course they never asked for a dispensation. Well why would they not knowing? Only then they discovered they were related. She was all for telling the priest. But that oul' bastard threatened to do her in. He wanted no truck with priests or his business made known. A gouger of the first order. She's afraid of her life of him. And as for the other—he's at her morning, noon and night. Nurse Gannon told me after every one of her children is born he's only waiting to pounce on her. The poor creature knowing every one of her children is born a bastard because they weren't married in the sight of God.'

'Unfortunate women,' my aunt said. 'One half living in dread and fear of their husbands and the other half of the priests.'

'She goes to the altar. I've seen her receive. That's a sacrilege,' the newcomer said.

My aunt gave her a scathing look and said, 'I'd let God be the judge of that ma'am, not you.'

Sacrilege. The word struck fear in my heart, bringing with it visions of hell. I didn't want to listen anymore and asked permission to go out to play.

ELEVEN

Through two more years we seemed to prosper—my sister growing into a toddler and my brother a well-established schoolboy.

God had been good to her, my mother frequently said both to herself and in conversation with her sister and neighbours. He had made my father turn over a new leaf. A house would be great but there were thousands in worse straits. You had to be thankful. And though she had lost the child, please God, if it was His Will she would be blessed with another. Sometimes this part of the conversation would lead my mother to suggest to her sister who was childless that she go down to the Coombe and have herself seen to. And my aunt would retort 'What, and have myself pulled about by a crowd of medical students. I'll do no such thing.'

And my mother would say, 'I suppose you've left it too late anyway.'

'What do you mean too late?'

'You're pushing forty.'

'So are you and you're talking about being blessed with another child.'

'The bloody cheek of you—I'm years younger than you.'

'Not that many.'

'I am so. My mother always said you were a big young wan when I was born.'

'Who are you coddin'—I know your age—you're a year and ten months younger than me—pushin' forty.'

'Forget it,' my mother would say and busy herself doing something and my aunt behind her back would wink at me.

Sometimes in the evenings if my father was working late my mother sat by the open window and watched people passing, and I would stand beside her as she reminisced about her youth. How she had been reared in the house opposite. What a happy childhood she had had. And how when she grew up she was the best-dressed girl in the street.

'I was mad about style and would pay the highest penny for my boots and shoes. And I never wore a ready-made costume in my life.'

She described the silk and satin blouses, velvet skirts and a pongee silk coat that had been the talk of the neighbourhood. One evening while she talked about her style, her eyes smiling and a happy expression on her face I took notice of what she was wearing. An old green linen dress with a brown leaf pattern on it. One she had altered from an American parcel that had come years ago. I remembered her unpicking, recutting and sewing the new frock by hand. Knew that through constant wear and innumerable washings it had split several times under the arms and been repaired. She wore no silks and satins now, everything for herself was second-hand or passed on from her sister—even her slips and brassières. The straps were often too slack and it was my job to thread a piece of tape between them, draw them close together and on her instructions raise the tape until she said, 'Stop, now tie a bow in them,' which I did, smoothing it flat between her shoulder blades. And I wondered standing by the window with her if sometimes she felt sad when she remembered all the style she didn't have anymore.

Permanent waves were all the rage. Women who had worn their long hair in coils and buns suddenly appeared with shorn frizzed heads. Hairdressers put advertisements in their windows: 'Start a Perm Club. Free perms and commission.' One of our neighbours raised a club and asked my mother to join.

'A shilling a week—it's only ten bob. Maybe you'll get an early number—you'd look gorgeous with a perm.'

In the draw my mother picked number five.

'Your hair's lovely, leave it alone,' my father advised the night before the hairdressing appointment.

'Indeed it's not. Only oul' wans have long hair these days. Perms are all the rage,' my mother replied.

She took me with her in the morning. We got the bus to D'Olier Street and from there walked across O'Connell Bridge. The crowds were bigger than usual and a street photographer tried to take our picture.

'On my way back,' my mother promised, 'I'm in a hurry now.'

'It won't take a minute,' the man coaxed, his camera poised. She pushed past him and we crossed Bachelor's Walk and along by Elvery's, the Metropole and the GPO.

'In there the Rebellion started. I remember it well. A scorching day it was and everyone out in their best. And over there at the foot of the Pillar you should have seen the Lancers, they were mown down. Lord have mercy on them—and the lovely horses stone dead. You stop dragging your feet and keep your shoulders back.' She poked me between them.

The hairdressing salon was very warm and very busy. Everyone seemed to be having perms. Hanks of all shades of hair were snipped from the heads of women whose startled faces looked out of the mirrors and their hands rose to their shorn heads. Assistants talked to them reassuringly and pointed to the coloured cardboard picture-stands of women with short, wavy hair, who smiled alluringly, draped in furs and jewels. And the cropped women, once soothed, smiled and shrugged and submitted. My mother's remaining hair was lotioned and bound to wires hanging from a machine which was then plugged into an electric socket. It took a long time to make the wave permanent, while we waited and my mother's face got redder and redder. Tea and Marietta biscuits were served and every so often my mother enquired of a passing assistant, 'When will I be done?' and was assured that it wouldn't be long now.

Eventually she was unplugged, unwound, brushed and combed. Her hair hung in narrow corrugated folds. Her expression was less than delighted. The hairdresser held a hand mirror and showed her the back and sides. Admiring her new style, complimenting her on the quality of her hair, how well it took the perm.

'Yes,' my mother said, 'it's lovely, it's grand.'

The assistant brought our coats and my mother offered her a tip which she refused. The refusing and insisting went on for the required length of politeness, then the tip was accepted with thanks and the rejoiner 'You didn't have to.' My mother replied that she knew the difference tips made to someone's wages and the girl held her coat. My mother put on her hat and it wouldn't fit. 'Your hair's so thick and the perm gives it more body,' the assistant explained. 'Here let me do it.' She forced down the hat and pushed home the pin. The corrugated waves bulged out on either side.

'That's a show,' my mother said.

'It'll be grand tomorrow when it settles,' the assistant assured her.

'I'm destroyed,' my mother said going through Henry Street. 'What possessed me to have my lovely hair tampered with? I hope I meet no one I know.' She turned up the collar of her coat and walked so quickly I was running to keep up with her. On the bridge the photographer greeted us with his camera at the ready. My mother dodged past him. 'The bloody cheek of them fellas taking up the pavement,' she said as we hurried on to the bus stop.

My father laughed when he saw her and she was raging.

'The curse of God on them and their perms,' she said, as with a comb and water she tried to flatten the wild fuzziness. 'Is it really that bad?' she asked my father. And he said 'no'.

'You're only saying that.'

'No I'm not—it's not that bad.'

'Tell me the truth,' she urged.

When he couldn't be drawn further she accused him of thinking her hair was desperate looking.

'I won't be able to show my face outside the door—look at it.'

'It's not as bad as you think. I'll tell you what—put a dab of brilliantine on it, it'll smooth it down.'

She did and admitted it made an improvement. But swore that never again would anyone ever persuade her to go next or near a hairdresser. Fashion or no fashion she'd rather look like Methuselah than the way she did now. The wild kinks calmed and her hair grew longer and she admitted that the new style was easier to wash and dry and she no longer spent a fortune on hairpins that vanished God only knew where. Life for us all was nice and easy. No ominous premonitions that it might not always be so.

* * *

'That cough is worse—you never seem to be without one these days.' My father, who was sitting cleaning the bowl of his pipe, scraping it with his penknife and throwing the dottle into the fire, said it was nothing—a tickle in his throat, that was all.

'It's more than a tickle, I didn't close an eye last night listening to it. I'm going to give you cough medicine and before you get into bed have a drop of hot whiskey—there's half a Baby Power.'

In the morning he couldn't get up and complained of a pain in his side. My mother felt his forehead and said it was like a furnace.

'I think you should have the doctor.'

I was alarmed—the doctor only came if there was a serious illness. My father tried to persuade her that the doctor wasn't necessary.

'A day or two in bed and I'll be all right. You'll be handing over five shillings for him to tell me I have a cold.'

'All the same I'm going to get him. Run up you,' she said to me, 'and leave this message with the chemist for the doctor to call.'

My mother was straightening the bed and tidying the room when I came back. My father was sitting by the fire with a blanket around his shoulders. His long drawers were hitched up slightly and I noticed how white the skin on his legs was. So white that blue veins were visible, not the raised knotted ones like on my mother's legs, just the tracing of veins that you saw behind your wrist or on a baby's forehead. I wondered if there was a chance of me having the whole day off school. But after giving me a cup of tea and a cut of bread my mother wrote a note to excuse me for going in late. It felt strange but pleasant arriving in school after everyone else—the playground deserted, not another person walking up the slope; knocking on the classroom door and, once inside, the curious stares of the children, the nun's question after she had read the note. Feeling very important I went to my seat. For a while I was the centre of attention and greatly enjoyed it, but after a lesson of Irish and another of mental arithmetic my new-found status was forgotten and so was my father and the doctor's visit.

At lunchtime the table was laid as usual and my mother at the stove cooking.

'Your daddy had to go into hospital. Sit down and eat this,' she said, handing me a plate of food. 'I'm only after getting back.'

My brother came running up the stairs and flung open the

door. She repeated to him what she had told me.

'Pleurisy,' she added as she gave him his dinner, 'that's what ails him. Dry pleurisy. Thanks be to God that's all it is. I was afraid it might be pneumonia.'

She talked while she ate the small portion she had served herself on a saucer.

'I've no appetite. The smell of ether turns my stomach. He'll be grand though. He has a fine constitution. Never sick a day in his life. He had that weakness the day you made your communion but that was years ago. Pleurisy is nothing. Watch the time—you don't want to be late again for school.'

I took her words at face value and told the nun when she enquired about my father that he was grand and would probably be home next week. She appeared to be delighted too.

'No,' my mother said when after school my brother and I asked if we could visit my father that evening. 'He needs rest, but definitely tomorrow.'

There was an air of excitement as she washed and dressed for the visit—the way it was whenever she was going out at night. She packed sweets, biscuits and some sandwiches to take to him. 'He won't like the food in there—he'll be starving. I wonder if I'm forgetting anything. I'll be straight home and you be good for Kitty. I think I'll buy him two ounces of Bulls' Eyes as well.'

After the visit she was in great humour.

'You could see the improvement in him and the comfort he's in. God bless the Protestant hospitals. And the nurses are little ladies.'

The following night we went with her. It was the first time I had ever been in a hospital and the smell of what I supposed was ether made me feel sick. And for the first time since my father's illness I felt apprehensive. I had never been in a building so big. The colours were dark and gloomy, dark brown wainscotting, olive green walls and in the large hall marble busts of old men. My aunt, uncle and a man who worked with my father were there. They all carried brown paper bags bulging with fruit and the man also had a syphon of soda water. We waited for permission to visit—the grown-ups talking in subdued voices. There was a porter in a little room and nurses, some with small head-dresses and an occasional one with a longer veil-like one, coming and going. The porter announced that visiting had started and we went up the wide wooden staircase with a carved bannister. My nameless fear increased as we followed my mother along a corridor.

The ward was enormous. I had never seen so many beds or such shiny brown oilclothed floors.

'There he is, there's your daddy, wave to him,' my mother said as we walked down the room.

Now and then she and her sister nodded or spoke to some patient in a bed we were passing. And later around my father's bed discussed who the men were. Neighbours, someone they had worked with, husbands, brothers or parents of friends. My father looked like himself and suddenly I wasn't afraid anymore. We kissed him and hugged him and he asked how we were. The grown-ups asked how he was feeling and he said he was grand. The man from work said he wouldn't mind changing places with him and everyone laughed. On his locker there was a dark-blue glass jar with a lid.

'What's that for?' I wanted to know.

'Don't ask so many questions,' my mother replied.

The grown-ups were talking about things I couldn't understand. I grew bored and looked around for something to interest me. At the bottom of my father's bed hung his chart. Gradually I inched my way down to examine it. There was only his name written on it and a squiggly red line with figures inked onto the squared paper. I was about to touch it when my mother spotted me and coming to the foot of the bed hissed in a low voice, 'Don't you dare. That's only for the doctor and nurse to handle—you're not even supposed to look at it.'

The visitors left before us.

'Take all that stuff home,' my father said, pointing to the bags that had been put on and in his locker. 'Only leave the soda water, I get very thirsty.'

We kissed him and promised when he asked that we would be good. He held my mother's two hands when she kissed him.

When I came in from school the following afternoon my aunt was there and my mother's face looked as if she was in bad humour.

'Are we going to the hospital again tonight?' I asked.

'No love,' my aunt said. 'Your mammy went this afternoon.'

'Oh,' I said, 'That's not fair, I want to go.'

'Sit over for your tea,' my mother said. She poured tea for herself and her sister and continued with a conversation I could tell had been interrupted by my arrival.

'I don't care what the X-ray shows, there's no foundation in it. None whatsoever. You only have to look at him. A fool could tell that. A man that never had a day's illness in his life. Did you ever hear anything like it—go out to a sanatorium. Out to Crooksling and lie on the flat of his back for six months! Well, I'm telling you this, they're as far out as the wind that blew their first shirt, if they think we'll take that advice.'

I listened. I knew about Crooksling. People with consumption went there. It was out in the country. The fresh air was supposed to make you better. Only it didn't. A lot of people who went there died. People who lived in the street. People I knew. Sometimes after six months they came home fat and rosy-cheeked. Sometimes only their coffins came in a hearse to be driven past their homes on the day they were being buried. Of the ones who came home I had heard my mother and the neighbours say, 'Blown out, that's all they are. Blown out on milk and butter and new laid eggs. How long will that last with no work to go to and nothing coming in? How long will that last on bread and butter and tea and margarine? The flesh will fall off of them when it's condensed milk they're drinking. Lookit—you can see them any day of the week—walking skeletons. The signs are all there, more pronounced on a man—his neckbones like a number eleven and once you see that, Mount Jerome's the next stop.'

I couldn't swallow my bread, it went so far and then stuck in my throat.

'Mind you,' said my aunt, 'Crooksling's not as bad as the Pigeon House. I wouldn't hear tell of anyone belonging to me going out to the Pigeon House. He can't be that bad or they wouldn't have recommended Crooksling.'

'He's not going anywhere. There's nothing wrong with him. And don't you go mouthing out of you that there is. I never want to hear what they say is wrong with him mentioned—do you hear me?'

'He's not well all the same.'

'He's got asthma—nothing more. You can live to be ninety with asthma. And not one point a finger or shun you. Asthma—that's what he's got.'

Then she noticed that my tea hadn't been drunk.

'You can't drink that—it's gone cold. I'll pour you another sup.'

She took my cup and emptied it. When she turned from the slop-bucket she was crying.

'It's not fair. He's only a young man. I wish I'd never sent for the doctor. Pleurisy, says he, stretching his hand for the two half-crowns, when all that ailed him was a heavy cold. I should have kept him at home. Not let him be pulled and hauled about and the life frightened out of him.'

She gave me my cup of tea and a couple of fig rolls sent home from the hospital by my father.

'A bloody little cur that doctor is. An insulting pup.'

'What else did he say?' asked my aunt.

My mother was drumming the fingers of one hand on the table, a preoccupied expression on her face and didn't answer my aunt's question.

'How do you mean he insulted him?' she tried again.

'I'll tell you how,' my mother replied, coming back from wherever her thoughts had taken her. 'While he was examining his chest he ordered him to turn his head away and keep his mouth closed. But that wasn't the worst; that only showed his pig's manner. What he said after showed his callousness.'

'What was that?'

'Jack said that even if there was anything wrong with him, which there isn't, how could he give up work for six months? Who would keep his wife and children? He told him that his eldest wouldn't be old enough to work for years. And that little bastard said, "If you refuse the treatment you'll never live to see her working."'

'All the same, I don't like the sound of it. Remember the pains in his chest and you told me yourself the sweat spills off of him in the night.'

'Asthma, that's what ails him, nothing else at all. And in any case there's nothing definite yet—they have to do another test.'

'Oh, what's that?'

'That little blue jar on the locker—that's a sputum cup. What he spits up has to be tested to see if it's positive or negative. It'll be nothing, nothing that a rest and strengthening-bottle won't cure. And as for that little dannyman of a doctor, God spoke before him. Jack'll live to see her and the other two grow up and for years after that.'

TWELVE

'My mother and father wouldn't do that—nor the King and Queen!'

I was aghast.

'They do so, honest to God. That's how women get babies,' Hannah said and scratched her head.

We were sitting on the steps of the big tenement house where Hannah lived. The sun was shining and the granite step was hot under my thighs. I wriggled and tugged at my very short dress to protect them.

'Your mother shouldn't make them that short, then you wouldn't get into trouble with the nuns,' said Hannah, whose hem streeled to her calves.

'Shirley Temple wears her clothes short. I'm going to have a Shirley Temple dress, a button-through one and a Shirley Temple perm,' I lied.

'Sister Eucharia said you're very immodest wearing short skirts and sleeveless dresses. What does that mean?'

I had to admit that I didn't know.

'I bet you were raging when she pinned paper round the hem of your dress. What did your mother say when she went down the next day?'

'That if she ever did that again I'd be taken out of the convent and sent to a Protestant school.'

'You'd go to hell then.'

We stopped talking and watched the people passing. I was thinking about what Hannah had told me. While I was pondering why anyone should do such a horrible thing, Hannah said, 'Eh, look, there's Rosie Apple. Will we folly her?'

Rosie Apple, an old Jewish woman, hobbled past and Hannah, to the tune of 'Yankee Doodle Dandy', chanted, 'Rosie

Apple went to chapel riding on a pony, Get two sticks and knock her down and make her stand aloney'.

'She's going to the dealers for her fish,' she said. We'll have a laugh. Come on, will we?'

I was thinking about the King and Queen. I loved the King and Queen and the princesses. I had listened to the programme about their coronation and seen the pictures of them in their beautiful robes and crowns. I closed my eyes and could see them again. Hannah, I decided, was a liar—they would never do dirty things like that—not the King and Queen. Having reached this conclusion I wasn't interested any longer in the news Hannah had imparted and changed my mind about tormenting Rosie, it would be a bit of gas. But by the time we caught up with her she was at the corner of Lombard Street where the fish dealers had their stock set out on boards across old prams and wooden carts; herrings and mackerel, cod and haddock, plaice and skate, the fishes' eyes and scales dimmed, their bodies flaccid and beginning to smell after hours in the sun. Rosie was buying fish and left with another woman—one who knew my mother and would lose no time telling me off and then letting my mother know I was annoying a poor unfortunate oul' wan.

'We'd better not,' I told Hannah. 'And anyway if we did Rosie mightn't let me light the gas on Saturday and I want all the pennies—I'm saving up to buy a Shirley Temple cut-out book.'

We went back to the steps where we talked and laughed, and every so often were so amused with ourselves that we had giggling fits in which we rocked and pushed against each other, our bodies close, and Hannah's long hair swung round her and touched mine.

'You're walking alive,' my mother said the next weekend when she fine-combed my hair. I knelt before her, my head over a piece of white sheet draped across her lap onto which fell generations of lice: the mother of them all, big, sated and dark-grey, younger ones paler in colour and the infants so pale and minute as to be almost invisible. One after the other my mother cracked them between her thumbnails. Afterwards my hair was washed and Harrison's Pomade rubbed in.

Lice, fleas and bugs were endemic. It wasn't unusual to see lice crawling on people in a bus, in mass, on the faces of a corpse. Fleas were gone before you saw them, leaving behind their small red bites. And bugs, if not already nesting behind the layer upon layer of wallpaper, came into one's home in second-hand furniture.

My mother waged constant war on the vermin. Regular fine-combing and inspection of hair. Wooden joints of bed-springs were sponged with paraffin oil. And flea hunting a routine. Disturbed in the bedclothes they burrowed into the fleece of the blankets or hopped so high that it was difficult to capture and kill them. Today the house would be vermin free and tomorrow a casual contact in school, on a bus, at the cinema or in a crowd, and the fleas and lice were back again.

Porridge, rice and all cereals had to be examined in case mice droppings had spoiled them, and not a crumb of bread left on the floor to encourage the mice. All these precautions and measures were part of running a home in a tenement. Constant vigilance and hard work.

'A match should be put to every one of the vermin-infested burrows,' my mother said, and prayed all the harder to St Jude for a clean new house.

***

The spring was cold and wet. For several days running my father got soaked driving the hearse. The weighty overcoat was difficult to dry. Even after being draped over a chair in front of a built-up fire it was still damp the following morning.

'If only you had two—one to change the other,' said my mother, holding the coat against her cheek to test its dryness. By the end of the week he was ill again.

'We'll have to get the doctor,' my mother said.

'You won't. I'll be better in the morning. Anyway you can't call the same doctor.'

'Why not?'

'He knows what's wrong with me.'

'There's nothing wrong with you that a week or ten days in hospital won't cure. He's not the only doctor—there's others with beds in different hospitals.'

'There's no need—will you listen to me.' He had a spasm of coughing.

'I am listening to you. We'll get another doctor.'

I was listening too and the knot in my stomach tightened.

It took several days for the routine tests to confirm again my father's tuberculosis and another few spent by a consultant more humane and compassionate than the previous one urging him to go to a sanatorium. In the meantime he had bed-rest and palliative medicines and afterwards was, he felt, well enough to go back to work. But this time there was a follow-up from the Health Department.

'How dare they pry into my business? But I'll soon put a stop to it. First thing in the morning I'm down to the Health Department. That nurse won't knock on my door again in a hurry.'

'Once your name goes on their list they folly you,' said my aunt who had come with a parcel of groceries in case my mother was feeling the pinch of my father having been out of work.

'Thanks very much.' My mother was unpacking the groceries. 'But there was no need. I wasn't short.'

'Feck you. I didn't say whether you were or not. If you don't eat the stuff do what you like with it. Your independence will be the cause of killing you.'

My mother ignored all this and carried on with what she had been saying about the nurse's visit.

'They won't folly me. The bloody cheek of her. Telling me I should have a separate bed. "Are you married?" I asked her. "No," sez she. "Well then what would you know about sleeping with a husband or the hurtful thing it would be for him if I didn't? And what gives you the right to come here dictating to me?" "It's your health and the childrens' I'm concerned about. Can I come in?" sez she. I kept the door in my hand. "Your husband is suffering from ..." I nearly dragged her into the room. "Do you mind not discussing my affairs on the landing. And for your information my husband is suffering from nothing but asthma. She drew in her horns then—changed her tune immediately. "I had to call. I was given your name and address. I'm sorry if I came at an inconvenient time." "That's all right," I said. She didn't have a bad face, a nice expression off her eyes. "Well, I won't delay you but while I'm here I might as well tell you what I'm supposed to." I needn't tell you I could feel my hackles rising again but I let her speak. "The children will have to be X-rayed, you'll be sent word. And there's free cod-liver oil from the dispensary at the back of the Meath Hospital. You might as well take it. It's very good for the children, puts fine limbs on them and great for chest complaints—it greases the tubes.'"

'I hope you've seen the last of her,' my aunt said.

'She won't darken this door again, not after the reception she got. Concerned about my health and the children's. Anyone would think he had leprosy or the smallpox. And the children are going next nor near no hospital—their lungs are as sound as a bell. Fine healthy children, God bless and spare them.'

She went on and on repeating the same fact, altering the phrasing of it in the hope of allaying her fears. She didn't succeed for I noticed, though my father never did, that she kept a separate set of cutlery and a cup for him which was regularly scalded. And when the card came with our hospital appointment—although she again ranted and raved about people's interference in her private life and that she was keeping no appointment—on the day we went. To her delight and relief we were found to be sound as bells. And shortly afterwards she decided that there was no harm in trying the cod-liver oil.

Up the narrow gravel laurel-edged path I walked. My heart in my mouth at the thought of going into the TB dispensary, of having any more to do with hospitals. There were cages of guinea-pigs where the path widened and I was reminded how once my father had explained to me what vivisection was. I stopped to look at the little animals and shuddered.

There were men and women sitting on long wooden benches waiting their turn to go to the hatch and be served with the cod-liver oil. They moved up to make room for me. A thin man with very bright eyes, his cheek bones red, asked me in a hoarse voice who was sick, my mammy or my daddy? I told him and he said I was a good girl. When his turn came to go to the hatch I looked after him and saw the number eleven on his neck. Once a week I was sent to the dispensary. I never saw the man again and wondered if he was in Mount Jerome. My mother always had a word of praise for how quick I had been. Sometimes she asked if there had been many people there. I'd tell her that, but never anything of my fears and loathing. How when I arrived at the gates I ran all the way to the dispensary, never looking towards the guinea-pigs; trying not to look at the necks of men waiting for their medicine, not to notice the horrible smells, the thin faces and bodies or hear the short staccato coughing that reminded me of my father. And never, never believing that one day he might look like the men and have the number eleven on the back of his neck.

He looked marvellous. Everyone said so and my mother put it down to the fact that there was nothing wrong with him and that the cod-liver oil was a great strengthener. I watched his face when he wasn't looking—it looked as it always had. He still came whistling up the stairs. He hooshed my sister up in the air and laughed and joked with me and my brother and when the wireless played nice songs put his arm around my mother and danced her round the room. So that sometimes for days I could forget that he was sick, that I had to go to the dispensary. But always my turn came round again.

* * *

'A waste of time and money,' my mother declared when I asked for the ingredients for rice pudding and a piedish. 'And for another thing you're not taking my good piedish.'

In an old enamel dish with scorch marks inside and out and slightly chipped on the corners I carried the ingredients to school and went to my first cookery lesson. The grey gas cookers were spotless, their metal taps gleamed, the tables and draining boards were dazzlingly white, not a speck of dust or grease anywhere. The cleanliness was intimidating, like the face of the cookery teacher which had a scoured look as if the coarse white sand used for scrubbing the woodwork was applied to it night and morning. She had sharp features, a sharp voice, and soon I was to learn that her knuckles too were sharp when applied behind my shoulderblades.

The ingredients required and the method for making a rice pudding had to be copied into our exercise books, then the preparations began. While the puddings were cooking the following week's recipe was written down and then we practised scrubbing with the grain. 'With your two hands, like that, hold the brush like that and scrub with the grain. What's the matter with you, are you deaf?' I felt her knuckles in my back, then she moved onto the next table.

The smell of rice and milk and nutmeg filled the room. Using an oven glove the likes of which I had never seen, for my mother used anything that came to hand to lift hot dishes from our cooker, I lifted out my pudding and put it with the others on a table to cool. I'd been liberal with the nutmeg so that the crust was a deeper golden brown than the others—I liked rice puddings that way. I waited to be allowed to collect it. Run all the way home, show it to my mother and say it wasn't to be touched until my father came home.

'Whose is this?' The nun's red-skinned finger pointed at my pudding.

I eagerly claimed it and waited for the praise which was sure to follow.

'How did I miss that filthy disgusting dish? Girls, com'ere. Look at that. Look at the dirt of that vessel. Did you ever see anything like it?' Her skinny pinched face was red with vexation, her voice shrill. She picked up the piedish with a look of disgust at having to handle such an offensive object. 'If I had seen that,' she said holding it up so that it could be seen by all, 'If I'd caught a glimpse of that you wouldn't have been allowed to use it in my kitchen.'

I had never liked this nun, now I hated her. I wished for something terrible to happen to her. I hated and hated her for making little of me, of my home, of my mother.

'Take it away,' she ordered. The effort not to cry, not to give her that satisfaction was so great that my hands shook as I lifted the dish. 'That's right,' she said, 'now drop it—go on you clumsy child. Spill it all over the floor. Get it out of my sight.' I was too hurt by the incident to complain to my mother about the nun.

'It's very nice,' my mother said when she tasted it, and my father said it was delicious. They both wanted to know why I wasn't eating it.

At the following cookery lesson I made soda bread which was the best in the class and the same nun praised its texture and how it had risen. Another unfortunate child got the sharp edge of her tongue. But the praise meant little to me. I never enjoyed another cookery lesson or forgave the nun for having humiliated me. Fortunately I didn't have to endure many more. The TB nurse came again. This time, tactfully not mentioning separate beds or specifying why, she told my mother that the Corporation was prepared to give her priority on the housing list. If my mother was agreeable all that was required was a letter from my father's doctor and a house would be offered.

'I have St Jude to thank for that,' my mother said, after

excitedly announcing the news at teatime. 'I knew he wouldn't let me down.'

She urged my father to get the letter as soon as possible.

'Just think of it—a house of our own, proper sleeping accommodation and not having to share the lavatory. I can't wait to get out of here. The day I go I'll light a bonfire under it.'

'Not very convenient for her next door,' my father said, laughing.

'Oh God—I never gave her a thought and she higher on the list—she'll be raging. I wonder what she'll say?'

'That the Corporation is full of ex-IRA men and one of them is a relation of yours.'

Taking him seriously my mother replied indignantly, 'How could she say that about us? Doesn't she know well everyone belonging to me was in the British Army? Don't we wear a poppy the same as herself?'

'I was only joking. But all the same she'll go down the minute she hears we've a house. She'll want to know why. I don't care for myself—but I thought I'd warn you.'

'They wouldn't divulge anything. Health reasons, that's all the information she'll get. It's confidential,' she said, deluding herself as she did when pawning in her single name. Ignoring the fact that the neighbour who heard everything that went on in our house above a whisper also heard my father coughing and like everyone else in Dublin at that time knew what such persistent coughing meant. And if she needed further proof it was there before her eyes on the day she met me coming out of the TB dispensary clutching the bottle of cod-liver oil which, for all that it was wrapped in the brown paper my mother sent with me, was nevertheless a bottle from the place that only dispensed for consumption.

The letter from the doctor was sent to the Corporation and every day my mother waited for word that a house had been allocated. And every night the conversation round the tea-table was of the new house and what the move would involve. The money that would be needed for the removal. What to take and what could be discarded. Where would we go to school? Was there a chapel within walking distance?

My mother wondered if we might get a parlour house. Parlour houses cost ten shillings a week, but for the extra half-a-crown look what you got—a nice little front-room and a separate bathroom—and usually parlour houses were semi-detatched.

'Ten shillings is twice the price of here,' my father reminded her.

Optimistically she brushed this warning aside. It could be afforded. It was worth every penny for the comfort you'd be getting. One way or the other we'd be paying more rent than for the room—an extra half-a-crown a week wouldn't beggar us. And with a semi-detatched you only have the one family to contend with. After all in a new scheme of houses you'd never know who could be living on either side of you. With God's help she'd get a parlour.

She didn't, but soon got over her disappointment when she saw the one allocated. We went to see it when my father came home from work. All of us as happy and excited as if we were on an outing to the seaside or going on a picnic in the country.

'Smell the fresh air,' my mother said as we picked our way over unfinished roads and stumbled on piles of building material by houses in various states of construction.

The house was an end one on a block of four. My mother was delighted with its outward appearance, the steps up to it, the front garden and long side gardens. The green hall door with its brass knocker, handle and letterbox.

'It's a little beauty. I'll make a rockery each side of the steps and we can grow our own vegetables. And it's a small road—you won't feel so lost on a small road.'

My father reminded her that it would be a good idea to see the inside of it. That if she didn't it would be getting dark soon.

'We have a torch,' my mother said, going round to inspect the back garden.

'I forgot it.'

'You bloody eejit—I told you to bring it.' She nearly got annoyed but once inside her good humour was restored, exclaiming at the size of the living-room, the combined scullery and kitchen. Able even to accept that the bath was there, too.

'It's a pity about that, but the hinged lid is a good idea, you could make it look like a table.'

My brother and I raced from room to room, ran up and down the stairs, in and out of the back door and kept asking, 'Is it all ours, do we own it all?' then ran up and down the stairs again. Until the noise on the uncovered stairs gave my mother a headache and we were ordered to stay still while she took the windows' measurements for curtains.

'The first thing I'll have to get is cross curtains. I couldn't live anywhere with everyone able to look in.'

Into his red-covered notebook my father wrote the measurements she called out, the notebook into which he copied favourite poems and the names of racehorses tipped as winners.

'Is it all ours?' I asked again.

'Every bit and please God we'll be happy in it,' said my mother, uncorking a bottle of holy water and splashing it about, doing her own blessing. Tired and happy, we caught a bus and went home, my mother still making plans. Tomorrow night she would go again and this time make sure of the torch. And she would bring coal and light the fire to give the place a bit of an airing.

I lay in bed and thought about the house. Remembering the new clean smells of wood and plaster, the doors with flat shiny paint that didn't have cracks and bubbles that peeled and showed the other colours beneath them. We would grow flowers in the garden, wallflowers with velvety petals, yellow and orange and dark red, and I'd bring bunches of them to school for the altar.

The gaslight was turned low and my mother and father sat by the fire. I saw him move his chair close to hers and put an arm round her and heard him say, 'Well, you've got your house. Are you happy now?'

'Yes,' she said, 'only I didn't want it this way. I'd have stayed here for ever and never grumbled, if instead of my little mansion, you had your health.'

She cried and he comforted her, telling her not to cry, not to worry, he felt marvellous. There was nothing wrong with him. There was nothing to cry for.

THIRTEEN

In the beginning we were as happy in the new house as my mother had hoped. The chapel was within walking distance. A new school was being built; in the meantime we attended the village school—a one storey, two-roomed building with only two teachers. Babies and small children were taught in one classroom, those between eleven and fourteen, the age of leaving, in the other. My father worried that our education would suffer with this arrangement, but my mother, on her wave of euphoria, assured him that for the little while we'd be there it wouldn't make much difference.

She constantly extolled the virtues of the new house and admitted that the Corporation scheme wasn't as bad as she had feared. Our road was small—only thirty-two houses. Filled by decent respectable people, not a bowsie or blackguard amongst them. Some she knew already—had worked with them, danced with them, or recognised them from knocking about town when she was single. But no one took liberties with her. She didn't like people dropping in and taking you unawares unless they were life-long friends.

You could feel the fresh air doing you good, she said. Between that and the proper sleeping accommodation my father was a new man. Able to walk the four miles to work, and with the garden dug, manured, and ready for planting in the spring.

She had a line that stretched from one end of the back garden to the other, a proper line with pulleys that sent the clothes high in the sky where they dried in no time and came in smelling fresh and clean. No more were the arms wrenched out of her carrying buckets of water up and down the stairs. No more passers-by walked through the hall to use the lavatory. She couldn't be happier. She had her house with a shut hall door.

But all too soon the disadvantages of the move from the city dawned on her. Living in the new house became expensive compared to living in the street. Everything bought in the local shops cost more. The loan for the removal van was being paid back. The minimum furnishing of four rooms, then lighting and heating them swallowed up my father's wages. In bad weather there were bus-fares as well. And in emergencies no-one to borrow a loan from until the weekend, so that the next time my father was ill there wasn't money for a private doctor and the dispensary one had to be called. His beds were in the Union Hospital and there my father was sent.

'That kip of a place—to think he's finished up there. My husband in the union!' my mother kept saying after the ambulance left. 'If I'd been in the street I could have run with something to the pawn. I could have borrowed the five shillings from anyone. Even if I'd lower myself to do it who'd have five shillings here? Everyone like myself living from hand to mouth.'

The next day after school I went to see my father.

'Take in these clean clothes and tell him I'll be down tonight. I'm sure he wanted something else. What was it? What did he say to bring in—maybe it'll come to me before this evening. Go on you.'

It was a nice day and the walk pleasant. I went through road after road of houses the same as ours and then passed modest new private ones which appeared sumptuous to me with their bay windows, well-tended gardens, white garden ornaments and newly planted trees. I was always apprehensive hospital visiting but was looking forward to seeing my father and it was such a lovely day that it was easy to keep the apprehension under control. Until I went into the Union grounds. I knew that paupers were housed there and had heard that a dog shouldn't be kept as they were. But I had never been inside the grounds before or seen a pauper. They were sitting in the sun, men and women all looking very old, dressed in rough dark-grey clothes, huddled on benches, the men and women seated in different courtyards. They said or did nothing to me as I passed and yet the sight of them, the smell of their clothes and strong tobacco, their eyes staring at me and the stillness of them made me tremble.

The hospital, once part of the workhouse, was bleak and comfortless, devoid of colour or decoration except for large holy pictures and life-sized statues of saints. The stairs up to the ward were stone and the bannisters iron railings. And everywhere the horrible smell of poverty.

Nursing nuns were in charge—assisted by able-bodied paupers on the male wards. My father was the only patient sitting up in bed. He looked all right and was delighted to see me. I kissed him and gave him the bag my mother had sent. He told me he was having the usual tests and medicine for his cough. And that he wouldn't stay a minute longer than he had to. Once his legs would support him and he got rid of the weight in his chest he'd be home. He took the clean under-clothes from the bag, some sweets which he gave to me, and said, 'She forgot the bread and butter. We could have had it with the cup of tea they'll bring round in a minute.'

Soon afterwards a big man dressed in the dark-grey clothes, his face stubbly, came into the ward with a trolley. Heads looked over the sheets and bodies hoisted themselves up in their beds.

'Most of them sleep between meals,' my father said, and laughed.

The trolley was pushed to his bed and the man handed him tea and bread. He reeked of string shag tobacco.

'Ther'yare Governor,' he said.

My father asked me if I was hungry. I said I was. I was always hungry. He shared the bread with me. The bread was grey and coarse-grained and smelled sour. I made a face.

'It's margarine as well,' my father said. 'Leave it and eat the sweets instead.'

Before I left he reminded me not to let my mother forget to bring in the bread and butter that evening. On the way down the stairs I saw the nun walking up to the ward. She ignored me. Her beads rattled as she passed. The tests showed the inevitable result, again the sanatorium was advised and refused. But this time my father wasn't fit enough to go home at the end of ten days. And as patients with tuberculosis weren't treated in the Union Hospital he was shifted to another one. My mother still referred euphemistically to his illness as being delicate, having a bad chest or poor health, though to close family, she did mention suggested treatments that might benefit him. And so I added 'gold injections' and 'pneumothorax' to my vocabulary. I also had a look at my father's chart one day when no staff were about. There was a lot more information on this one, including a diagram of a pair of lungs. Inside the left one was another diagram drawn in red ink and written by the side of it the word cavity. A hole in my father's lung! It was several weeks before he came home and several more before he felt strong enough to go back to work.

His employer had paid him the first two weeks wages, bringing them to the hospital. Then instead of money, gifts were sent, tobacco and giant jars of Horlicks. Workmates when they visited slipped him half-crowns, which he gave to my mother.

The sickness-benefit no where near made up for the loss of his wages and my mother was desperate for money. Something would turn up, God never closed one door without opening another. She had faith in abundance but in the meantime the milkman, the rent-man, the society-man and numerous other things, not the least being food, had to be payed for. She had an idea! My sister had been born with a caul. Cauls were in great demand by sailors, she said. If you had a caul you never drowned. Speculating on the five pounds a sailor would part with for one, she advertised in the evening paper. No one answered the advertisement. So in desperation she decided to pawn the sideboard. To sell would have brought more money, but pawned it was still hers. and something was bound to turn up before it 'went in the pawn'. She'd be sure to find the money and release it. It was dusted and polished before a young fella came with a handcart to bring it to the pawnbrokers.

'Anyway,' she said, as she watched it being pushed away, 'it was too big for this place.'

'As soon as I'm in work again we'll get it out,' my father promised. She prayed, the nuns in school prayed and I prayed, though less hopefully than I should. Unable to believe wholeheartedly in God's ability to perform miracles. For how could God get inside my father's body and mend the holes in his lungs? The prayers were answered as my mother never doubted they would be. My father got well enough to work and strong enough to plant vegetables and sometimes take us on walks as far as the Phoenix Park.

Gradually my mother got on her feet again, but the Sunday roasts became smaller, and sausages, only previously used for weekend breakfasts, were served once a week for dinner. And when the expiry date on the pledged sideboard arrived and there was no money to release it, my mother consoled herself by saying, 'It was only a bloody gazebo anyway.'

Her search for antiques were now a thing of the past. Food and warmth were the priorities, though she still regularly found pennies for us to pay at the pictures. And neighbours, as badly off as we were, never sent a child for a message without rewarding them with a copper. The poor helped the poor.

FOURTEEN

Walking to and from the village school I passed the new one being built. It was, rumour had it, the biggest and most modern in Europe. The playground would be on the roof, there was to be an assembly hall with a stage and balcony, playing fields and all sorts of marvellous things. I daydreamed about attending it. How wonderful it would be—like all the schools I read about in story-books and *Girl's Own*—but better because you could come home every night. Once, before the school opened, I heard my mother and father talking about it. She singing its praises. But my father said that for all its modernness it would give no more chance of a good education than any other National School. Too much Irish and Religion would be taught. And that he had it on good authority from a fella in the union that the nuns who would be teaching in it considered the children to be factory fodder. My mother said that that was the fruits of living in a scheme. Even though the majority living on the estate were hard-working, decent people with children as bright as anyone's, everyone would be tarred with the same brush. And no one was more guilty of that than the nuns.

My mother was forever rearranging the furniture now because without the sideboard the room looked bare. And she missed its storage space.

'I've nowhere to keep anything,' she complained. 'The place is like a rath.* Wasn't I an awful fool to let it go in the pawn. I'll never get an article like it again.' Then she'd cheer up and say, 'Ah well, let all my bad luck go with it. So long as we have our

* A prehistoric hill fort.

health that's the main thing.' And for months we all had our health.

It was very seldom that a car drove through the road—very seldom that any vehicle did except the milkman, coalman and the man who sold the vegetables. All had horse-drawn carts so the road was safe to play all the games in their seasons. Skipping and marbles and Queenie—where one girl stood with her back to the group and threw a ball over her head. It was caught and concealed, and everyone stood with hands clasped behind their backs chanting 'Queenie, Queenie, who has the ball?'

Our games required very little equipment. When we had no marbles or money to buy them we played buttons, robbing our mothers' stock, kneeling by the curb and shooting the buttons towards the wall, the one who shot the closest winning. Balls the size of tennis balls made from sponge or rubber gave the greatest enjoyment. They served for games of cricket played against a wicket chalked on the wall, for Rounders and Queenie and for the individual games in which some girls could keep balls going against a wall in rhythm to a chant, those who excelled keeping six in play. Then there was Piggy Beds. Long rectangles were chalked on the road, divided into sections and numbered, the top section being labelled Home. The Piggy was a polish tin, Cherry Blossom or Nugget, filled with clay. On one leg you hopped from bed to bed kicking the Piggy before you, the object of the game being to get Home without foot or Piggy landing on a chalk line. At Home you rested before beginning the return journey.

'Them bloody beds, I'll kill you so I will, look at the toe of your shoe,' my mother and everyone else's mother said during the Beds season, but still found us empty polish tins to make Piggies.

Beds went out and whip and tops came in and competition to decorate the tops was fierce. Diamonds, circles, squiggles, all sorts of patterns were painstakingly drawn on the small top's surface in coloured chalks or, better still, if coloured silver paper could be found it was stuck by spit in minute scraps to make a dazzling mosaic when from its wound-lash the top was released and spun, its momentum kept up by skilful application of the whip.

Then as suddenly as the games came in they went out and we explored the countryside which surrounded our estate. Finding the streams and water-filled quarries which we were forbidden by our parents to go near. Eating watercress that grew in abundance, and the bread and cheese blossoms of the may tree; collecting armfuls of cowslips, which our mothers buried their faces in when we brought them home; laying on our bellies to drink the water that flowed over pebbles for that, we believed, was the purest water of all. We ran and raced, leapt over streams, climbed trees and jumped obstacles. Breathless we flung ourselves on the soft green turf and closed our eyes against the sun. For then the sun always shone.

The school, when it opened, was like a dream come true. Everything was new and shiny; the windows, floors, doors and desks, even the inkwells unstained; the lavatories spotless. There were dozens and dozens of classrooms opening off long corridors, all large-windowed and flooded with light. There was an assembly hall as big as a picture house and it had a balcony and a proper stage.

Green fields surrounded the school. In the future these would be our playing fields. But in the meantime, we were told, our playground was on the roof. A very modern idea. We were lucky children to have such a wonderful school. It had cost a lot of money. It was hoped we would appreciate it, work hard and not do any damage.

The playing fields didn't materialize in my time but the roof area made an adequate playground for games of something like netball without the posts. To my delight we had teams and I was made a captain. I couldn't wait to go each day. Driving my mother mad with my demands. Money for books, brown paper to cover them, this dress and not the other one, clean hankies or their substitutes—old pieces of sheeting. Then spick and span and smelling of Palmolive soap I set off.

In the beginning every girl in my class was clean and tidy. But as time passed the impetus of a new start waned and girls came in creased dresses and skirts, in shoes that weren't polished, socks that were dirty with holes in the heels; without hankies, wiping their hands across their noses and getting into trouble with the nuns for being careless and untidy.

Almost everyone was poor. Some had as many as ten brothers and sisters. Most of them had idleness in the family, fathers on the labour or relief. Very few wore long warm brown woollen stockings or silk and satin ribbons in their hair, or brought money for the black babies or flowers galore for the altar. And so with my neat appearance, fluent reading, good speaking voice—and lack of nose picking or running—I stood out. Full of importance, trusted to go on messages and, at last, over the press.

And there was drama. Our first production opened with a tableau. Five girls dressed in art-silk robes wearing crowns. The tallest girl, who had long black hair, was Éire, and I was Leinster. After the tableau there was singing and dancing. Individual renderings of *Ave Maria* and *Panis Angelicus*. An old stout nun had prepared us for the dance routine, hitching up her skirts and teaching us to step-dance to 'Phil The Fluther's Ball' and a kind of soft shoe shuffle to 'Ten Pretty Maids at the Village School'.

On the night we were grease-painted and powdered. With palpitating heart and a desperate urge to pee I took my place on the dais. I could hear the audience, the shuffling of feet, the coughs, the talking. Waiting for the curtains to open was unbearable. And then they did and before me were millions of faces, heads and eyes. Were my parents there? Supposing they hadn't come. No one would know what I looked like or how well I recited my piece. Then I saw them and they were waving and I almost waved back. I was so excited, so proud of myself, so full of joy and so afraid I'd wet myself or slip from my dais. But I didn't and after my recitation got a great clap. And then I danced and never missed a step and kept time to the music. I made up my mind there and then I was going to be an actress—maybe a filmstar. But most of all I was determined to stay in school for ever and ever. I even worked hard at Irish and arithmetic, listened attentively to the teacher or nun, never missed my homework and was first to put my hand up for every question except those in Irish and mental arithmetic—then my brain became paralyzed.

I was so happy in school that for days on end I forgot that my father was sick with something from which he would never get better. So that only when without warning he had a convulsive bout of coughing did fear clutch at my heart, blotting out my happiness and forcing me to confront the outcome of his illness. Overwhelmed with sadness I'd go to my bedroom or into the garden, anywhere that he wouldn't see me crying, and ask why? One day when this happened I became angry with God who had made my lovely father sick and wouldn't or couldn't make him better. Perhaps couldn't because, like Father Christmas and the fairies, there was no God. It was an awful thought that had already flitted through my mind but which I had quickly banished by saying aspirations and thinking of something else. Now I dwelt on it and terrified myself. For if there was no God there was no heaven and if these things didn't exist then neither did souls. So if my father died where did he go? Into a coffin and into a grave. And then what? And if I died?

From that day onwards I was to retain my doubts. God couldn't do anything because there was no God. I didn't want to believe this. I wanted there to be a heaven and to go there when I died. I wanted my father to be there and one day we would all meet there as we were taught. I wondered if other children had these doubts. Had my mother? Did the nuns and priests have doubts? If only you could talk to someone. I could to my father but wouldn't for I'd have to explain why the doubts had arisen in the first place. And most of the time my father was happy-go-lucky, singing the latest songs, whistling 'Begin the Beguine', 'Sand In My Shoes'. How could I tell him I kept thinking about him dying. He was constantly planning the years ahead when, unless the war came, he would take me to England. Show me London and Brighton. The pier on which he had played as a boy, the plaque in his old school where his name was inscribed with those of other boys who had excelled. So my doubts and fears had to be coped with alone. Fortunately there were many distractions besides school.

FIFTEEN

The garden grew drills of potatoes, heads of salad and cabbage, scallions and beetroot. My father whistled and sang while he worked, digging and hoeing, earthing up the potato drills, dipping seedlings into liquid manure. It wasn't difficult to forget that he had been ill. The rockery my mother had planned on her first visit to the new house never materialized. She had her heart set on granite stones and had located a granite doorstep, one of several lying outside houses in the process of being built. 'That's the very thing,' she said, 'and sure the Corporation will never miss it—they've thousands of them.' St Jude must have come to her and my father's assistance on the night they pinched the stone, lending them the strength to hoist the doorstep on to the go-cart and push it home. But once there the heavenly assistance was withdrawn and all my father's attempts to do other than slightly chip it failed. So that for years the stone lay where it had been toppled from the push-chair and became a seat for us.

Bigger girls, sisters of my new friends, explained more explicitly than Hannah had done what men and women did to get babies. And now I no longer found it totally unbelievable. The big girls had breasts unbrassièred which bounced when they skipped and dark curly hair between their legs. It showed when they squatted in a field to pee and pulled back the leg of their knickers. They knew all sorts of things including where to get pennies for something they wanted.

'There's an oul' fella,' they told us, 'he'll give you a penny for pulling back the leg of your knickers. Honest to God.'

I went with them on a hot day to a lane on the outskirts of the estate. One side of the track was allotments and an orchard. Two small houses faced the orchard.

'There he is, the dirty oul' get,' one of the big girls said as we neared the house.

The man was old and fat. He wore a greasy-brimmed soft hat and his trousers were tied up with a length of string. He was leaning over the high iron gate scratching himself near his belly.

'Don't any of youse go too near, he might grab hold of you and murder youse,' a big girl warned.

The little girls with no hair to show moved into a group and we hung back while three big girls approached.

'Hello Mister,' they said.

The hedge beside the gate had white convolvulus growing in it and there were bees buzzing round the flowers. Apart from their sound it was very still and there was no one about except the man and ourselves and a big collie dog asleep by the door of the man's house.

'Hello Mister,' the big girls said again. 'Do you want to see it?'

The man nodded his head in its soft, greasy hat.

'Give us the money then?'

He made a sound in his throat and shook his head.

'There's no flies on that oul' fella. He may be mad but he remembers that we ran away last week without letting him see. We'd better hurry up, someone might come.'

The girl who spoke went nearer the gate and the other two followed. The man unbuttoned his flies. The girls lifted the summer dresses and pulled back the leg of their knickers. The man was patting himself. I moved round a girl to see what he was patting but there was nothing only dirty long drawers. His face got very red and sweat was on his grey stubble and all the time he was panting and patting. I thought he was going to have a fit.

'Hurry up,' a girl shouted. 'Hurry up and give us the money. If you don't we'll scream.'

He was in a fit I was sure, and now his eyes were closed and his mouth open. I could see his big thick tongue. Maybe he was dying. I'd never seen anyone dying. I stared at him. And then he went quiet and opened his eyes. He fastened his fly-buttons and then went into his pocket and peered at the coins he took out.

'The shaggin' oul' louser, he'll take all day making sure he has the right money. If anyone comes up the lane and sees us standing here we'll be in trouble. Will you hurry up,' the biggest of the girls said, going closer still to the man. 'There, them's pennies,' she pointed to his palm. And he took three out and threw them into the road. She picked up the money.

'Come on everyone, we'll buy apples. And if any of youse tell your mother we'll all be kilt. Say as true as God you won't.'

'As true as God,' we replied.

The woman in the orchard said it was a lovely day thanks be to God. And asked if we were good girls. We said we were and told her we were thirsty. She gave us water and bags of apples. Apples with leaves still on them, apples so delicious, so sourly sweetly crunchy, the juice ran down my chin and I ate every bit except the pips.

No one mentioned the old man or what they and he had done. I knew it was wrong, but told myself it was all right because I had only watched. And as for running home and telling my mother—I never told her anything that wasn't absolutely necessary, having long ago learned to lie about where I had been and what I had done during the summer holidays.

I went to forbidden play areas, to water that was deep and stagnant. Walked barefoot in cow manure, watching it squelch up through my toes, afterwards washing in a running stream. And spent hours playing on the Corporation's city dump. Poking through cinders and Vesuvius-like mounds of ash. Pushing dead cats, rags, bottles, bones, lumps of rubber, empty tin cans, torn mattresses aside in my search for treasure which one day I found in abundance. A chocolate factory had burned down and the bitter, burnt, smoky chocolate was tipped in tons on the dump. I ate it until my stomach felt ready to burst and still didn't feel sick. And would have gone on gorging it if I hadn't heard the Angelus and known I had better make my way home for a dinner I didn't want.

One afternoon when we had been living in the new house for some time my aunt came on one of her visits. Until her arrival I had been reading *Little Women:* captivated by the story, identifying with Jo, hating Beth and wishing that a boy like Laurie lived next door. Reluctantly I put the book away, first marking my page with one of my father's spills, for long ago my mother had told me that I must never turn down the corners of a page.

My aunt, while unpacking the gifts she had brought my mother, asked, 'What ails you? You're looking down in the mouth, you're not in the way again are you?'

My mother said no, she wasn't in the way and that nothing ailed her.

My aunt had brought a cake for tea, a bottle of cough medicine for my father, sweets for my sister and the *Dandy* and *Beano* for me and my brother. I curled up again in the chair to read my comic and while I pursued the adventures of Korky the Cat listened to the conversation.

'He hasn't started careering again?'

'That's you all over,' said my mother. 'Jumping to conclusions—you're very bad minded. Once he turned over a new leaf there was no hunker-sliding.'

'I'm glad to hear it,' my aunt said sarcastically. 'So what is it that ails you? Don't tell me you've fallen out of love with your house?'

'Not the house, I love the house, but I don't think I'll ever get used to the place. God knows I tried hard enough, but I miss the city. There was always something going on in the street. Fifty times a day you could look out of the window and see something or someone to interest you. But here you might as well be dead. Every house lick alike, every road the same. Miles and miles of grey pebble-dash. I'm telling you it's enough to send you out of your mind. And on an overcast day—well!'

'I wouldn't live here—not if I got a place for nothing. It's too far out and miles to the bus stop. And for another thing look at what it costs in bus-fares.'

'You can say that again. Between fares and paying through the nose for everything locally I'm robbed. I'm telling you if I could put the house up on a cart I'd be back in the street tomorrow.'

I was glad my mother couldn't do that. I was so happy with my new friends in my new school and surroundings that I never gave the street nor anyone in it a thought. And on the rare occasions when I did return there was delighted when it was time to go home again.

I loved the fact that we lived almost in the country. And besides that we had the pictures. Every Saturday afternoon I went, queuing with what appeared to be every other child from the estate who had the twopence entrance fee. And for a couple of hours we watched the films, sometimes Shirley Temple, Jane Withers or Deanna Durbin complete pictures. Other times the film, usually a Western, was a 'follyan upper'. Cowboys and Indians galloping across the prairie, chasing each other, catching each other, killing each other. We booed the Indians and cheered the cowboys, then sat in horrified silence when the

Indians burned down the whiteman's log cabin after first killing him and his wife, though the scalping, to our disappointment, was done off screen. Silently we prayed that the child who, doing the father's bidding, had hidden when it was known that the Indians were approaching, wouldn't be discovered. The sigh of relief that went up when the Indians rode off! Then along came a cowboy or a Colonel (the chap, in Dublin) who stared aghast at the scene before preparing to remount and ride after the marauders. Then changed his mind and began searching for survivors. Approaching to within inches the bushes or boulders behind which the child cowered. The audience roared: 'Over there. Look. You missed it. There. Behind you. Beside the tree. Are you shaggin' well blind?' A wail of anguish rose from our throats and hearts as the searchers once again prepared to mount. Frenzy broke loose—the audience standing, roaring. 'You passed her. Turn around. Go back, go back. Just over there.' And this time they heard us and followed our directions, found the child, now unconscious, one arm stretched out within inches of a rattlesnake poised to strike.

The lights went up—the spell was broken. But the adrenalin still surged, and boys, for no apparant reason, punched boys and girls alike, called each other names and threatened to dye the other's eye. They rolled around in the sweet-paper-strewn aisle mauling each other and the girls screamed in pretended terror. Then all the exit doors were flung open and the attendants cleared us out.

For the rest of the week the picture was retold and re-enacted by a boy with the gift of the gab who could take off American accents and was fast on the draw of an imaginary pistol. Girls were tolerated on the edge of the group only. In any mixed activity boys were always the bosses. But all the same I was discovering that boys were nice. Different. More exciting to play with if the game involved a chase. It was thrilling to be captured by a boy and dragged pretending protest to the den. Boys arms and bodies didn't feel soft like girls' did and, for some reason that I didn't understand, that was nice too.

* * *

'I'll be killed! Mother Mary Jane Francis will murder me. It's Ash Wednesday and I haven't been for the Ashes.'

'If you don't stop bawling like a jackass I'll murder you. I was up half the night with your father, that's why I slept it out,' my mother said, rushing between the stove and the table, dishing out the breakfast.

'She won't take that for an excuse,' I whinged.

'Com'ere,' my mother said, putting down the porridge pot. 'Com'ere with me.'

I followed her into the living-room where she knelt by the fireplace.

'Keep your hair out of the way,' she said, rising from the grate and planting her ash-covered thumb on my forehead, smudging it sufficently to show beneath my fringe. 'Now eat your breakfast and no one will be the wiser whose hand gave you the ashes.'

Mother Mary Jane Francis, a strict but fair nun, wasn't there that morning. Sister Angela was instead. She inspected our foreheads and delivered another lecture on mortality. Repeating what the priest would have said at the giving of the Ashes, 'Dust thou art and unto dust thou shalt return. And make sure you remember that. Your body is nothing but a heap of corruption. Your soul is your most precious possession.'

Sister Angela looked like a white bull. She had a broad flat face and a body that was grossly overweight. Her podgy hands, when not pointing at a culprit, writing on the blackboard or joined in prayer, were concealed in the flowing sleeves of her robe where we knew she also held 'the leather', which resembled a short stiffened razor strap, and was produced with a flourish as an offender fearfully approached her. Then with passionate enjoyment she wielded it, a look of fierce concentration on her face, so bull-like that I half expected to see steam billow from her nostrils and her flat black shoe paw the floor.

But the stinging burning pain of the leather was short-lived. Unlike the malediction she had once called down upon the class when, during an exposition of the Blessed Sacrament, we had been overcome by an hysterical fit of laughter. The following morning, after failing to find out who started the infectious giggling, she cursed us: 'That the tongues of each and every one of you who laughed before the Blessed Sacrament may swell up in your mouths with cancer and choke the life out of you. Now bless yourselves. In the name of the Father and of the Son and of the Holy Ghost.' I closed my eyes and saw monstrous tongues, bigger than the ones in the butcher's brine barrels, purple, swollen, grotesque. I tried to swallow but couldn't.

But Sister Angela and her sadism was exceptional. The other nuns were kind, just and concerned not only with our spiritual welfare. They knew whose father wasn't working, which child needed the extra free milk and hot currant buns everyone was given. Looking out for bright children and offering free places in a secondary school run by the Order in another part of the city.

One day I was told that it might be possible for me to go there. Would I tell this to my mother and ask her to make an appointment to see the Reverend Mother. I was ecstatic and ran all the way home at lunchtime, my mind full of the uniform I would wear, the bus I would take to school each day, the hockey stick, maybe even a tennis racquet. The benefits of the academic advantages never occurring to me.

'Mammy, Mammy!'

'Don't be always rushing in like a lunatic. You nearly knocked the pan out of my hand and it full of scalding grayce.'

'I'm going to the secondary school. Honest to God. Sister Mary Jane Francis said. And you won't have to pay.'

'Did you ask Sister Mary Jane Francis who's going to keep you?'

'It costs nothing I told you.'

'You get nothing for nothing. I know you won't have to pay the fees. But there's the uniform, the bus-fare and the books. Move out of the way if you don't want to be scalded. Tell the nun "thanks very much" but that your mammy says she's waiting for you to be fourteen so you can start keeping yourself.'

'It's not fair. I want to go.'

'Don't you back answer me.'

There was a time when I seldom had but lately I often did. We seemed to disagree about so many things. She was always on at me. I couldn't help myself—I had to back answer.

'I'm warning you,' she said as I argued. 'And another thing, not a word about it to your father.'

'I will so tell him. He'll let me go. I know he will. You stop me from doing everything. No one else on the road has to be in as early as me or have their hair in an Eton crop. I hate it. I look like a gnome.'

'Take that,' she said clattering me across the face. 'And if you open your mouth again you'll regret it. You're still a child and you'll do as you're told.'

I was too hungry to do any play-acting about eating my dinner.

'Do you want another bit of a potato?' my mother asked.

Sullenly I refused.

'Turn your arse to it then.'

But silences never lasted long between us. I had noticed a peculiar looking bottle on the mantlepiece and, not being able to restrain my curiosity, asked: 'What's that?'

'Potter's Asthma Cure. It's suppose to be marvellous for congestion of the lungs. Did you not hear your father during the night? How he had the strength to go to work this morning I don't know.'

'I never heard him,' I said in a challenging tone.

'That's because you're young and can sleep through anything. But if you were lying beside him you would. He couldn't get his breath and the spills of sweat were drenching him. Wait'll I show you how the lamp works.' She lit it and the room smelled of burning hay. 'It's herbs, that's what the man in the chemist told me. It's grand for asthma.'

'He hasn't got asthma.' I took pleasure in contradicting her. 'I saw what he has—it was on his chart.'

'Finish your dinner and get back to school before I clatter the other side of your face. And tell your teacher I'll be up to see her and explain why you can't go to the secondary school. And I might enlighten her about what you're really like.'

Of course I knew without any doubt that my mother would never criticize one of her children to anyone.

'I'd go up to my neck in blood for each and every one of you', I had heard her say. And I think she would have. But that didn't stop me hating her on the way back to school or going over in my mind all the things she deprived me of. The restrictions put upon me, on how I should wear my hair, her choice when we went to buy socks or material for the dresses she made for me. And now another thought came to me. Maybe if she had been different my father would have gone to a sanatorium. And maybe he would have been one of the lucky ones who got better. Without knowing it I was to be critical of my mother for a very long time.

SIXTEEN

During 1936 my father agonized over what was happening in Spain and talked about joining the International Brigade. My mother paid little attention to him, having her own concern to agonize over. Poor Mrs Simpson and the King! Such a lovely couple, anyone could see how much in love they were. There was a man for you—ready to sacrifice everything for the woman he loved. She read everything she could find about the lovers, commenting that you couldn't call her a beauty, she was a bit flat-faced, but knew how to make the most of herself.

In the warm evenings I sometimes couldn't sleep, and listened to the crowd of young men who gathered at our corner. One had a mouth organ and another a melodeon. The sound of singing and music drifted in through the open window: 'In the Chapel in the Moonlight' which I thought was a beautiful song, everyone joining in, followed by 'It Happened in Monterey a Long Time Ago'. I wondered where Monterey was? The boy on the mouth organ played a piece I had heard Larry Adler playing on the wireless—'Stormy Weather'. I loved that as well. Sometimes on the nights they played if my mother and father had gone to bed early I could hear her giving out. Urging my father to go and tell them they were destroying her night's sleep and to get to hell's gates out of it. He wouldn't, saying that they were doing no harm, only killing time. Poor young fellas with no work, no money for a pint or the price of the pictures. It was a terrible state of affairs that some men had never known what it was to have a job. To the sounds of their voices and the singing I drifted to sleep. Nothing was ever mentioned again in school about my secondary education. But as a result of my mother's visit to the Reverend Mother I was discreetly given extra bottles of milk before I went home. They were a third of a pint, squat bottles with a cardboard top in the middle of which was a circle that could be pushed through and a straw inserted. There were no straws, so after poking my finger through I pulled off the cardboard, licking with relish the underside which was thick with cream—but only if there wasn't a nun about. Licking, eating and drinking at the same time was bad manners. Drinking with food in your mouth was something only pigs did.

Manners were high in the nuns' list of priorities. The class stood when the priest or another adult came into the classroom, you waited going up or coming down the stairs if a grown-up was ascending or descending. As the girls in my class neared puberty sexual morality was hinted at. We were approaching the age when soon we would be women. Our bodies were inviolate. We must never allow anyone to touch them in an immodest way. If there was anything troubling us or anything we wanted to know we were advised to ask our mothers or one of the Sisters.

Imagine, we said to each other afterwards, asking one of the nuns about anything like that, or your mother. We laughed embarrassedly at the thought and continued to piece together the facts of life from information passed on by girls who had older sisters menstruating. And more exciting though still puzzling information from those who had married sisters. Men do things to women to give them babies. It was a sin if you weren't married—a terrible sin. One girl told us that men were dirty oul' things. Anyway her sister's husband was. 'Guess what he wanted her to do on their first night?' she asked.

'What?'

'Stand in her skin so he could look at her.'

We were appalled.

'She locked herself in the wardrobe and he threatened that if she didn't come out he'd throw her and the wardrobe down the stairs.'

'And then what happened?' we asked all agog.

'Well she had to come out. But my mother says she'll send the priest on him if he doesn't change his ways.'

The following year we had a lay teacher. She was very pretty and pleasant, wore lovely clothes and was the first person to kindle my patriotism, which had until then been pledged to England, the King, Queen and the little princesses. Everything

English filled me with pride: the sound of Big Ben on the wireless, the newscaster's perfect speaking voice, 'God Save The King', 'Land of Hope and Glory', and the wearing of a poppy on Remembrance Day. From the new teacher I heard about ships on the Spanish Main bringing wine from the Royal Pope, and learnt Mangan's 'Dark Rosaleen'. I sat spellbound as I had when my father took me to the theatre, listening to every word, my eyes unable to leave the teacher's face. For me it was a performance comprising a lovely voice, words that conjured pictures, and a mesmeric musical quality. That there was an allegorical element to the poem I didn't know for some time, but when I learnt it by heart and recited it at home my father said I was being indoctrinated and my mother that the country was still in the grip of the IRA and every one of them in the top jobs or drawing fine pensions. From the same teacher I learned the poetry of Patrick Pearse and was greatly moved by the lines, 'I do not grudge them Lord, I do not grudge my two strong sons, That I have seen go out to break their strength and die, They and a few in bloody protest for a glorious thing. Oh Lord, thou art hard on mothers, We suffer in their coming and their going ...'.

Gradually I was able to place Patrick Pearse in the day's events of Easter Monday 1916 of which my mother often spoke, though never with regard to its political meaning.

Sometimes the poetry teacher sent me for a message. Writing a note for me to take to the chemist where I was handed in return a soft package wrapped in brown paper. Though never having seen sanitary towels even in their own wrapping I guessed that's what they were. For several months on and off I went on the errand. Then the errands stopped and I thought no more of it.

The poetry teacher grew cranky. One day she didn't come to school and we were told she was sick. Sometime afterwards a girl whose mother had a friend who lived next door to a friend who cleaned for the teacher told me that the teacher was going to have a baby and the nuns had got rid of her.

'That's why she stopped sending you to the chemist—she missed "the others".'

'Do you have a baby if you miss them?' I asked.

'Of course you do.'

'Without doing things with men?'

'I'm not sure. I'll ask my sister. Have you started yet?'

'No,' I said.

'Nor me. I wonder when we will?'

My father got sick again and went back into Rialto Hospital. He looked very ill now and so did everyone else in the ward. While he was in hospital my periods started one afternoon in school. I wasn't frightened and as it was nearly home time decided to wait and tell my mother rather than a nun. I noticed that there was a different smell from my body—not unpleasant, it reminded me of marrow.

'Thanks be to God,' my mother said when I told her. 'Delicacy sometimes delays them. I was worried about you.'

'But I'm not delicate.'

'Of course you're not,' my mother assured me and went on to tell me that a girl's periods were a gift of Our Lady making her into a woman.

'You're a lovely soft girl and from now on you have to mind yourself—never let a boy be free-making with you.'

And that was all except for telling me that though I must sponge myself every day I couldn't have a bath or wash my hair while I was losing. It would last for between five and seven days and come once a month. But the most important thing apart from minding myself was never ever to leave the cloths she would give me lying about and on no account to ever talk about my periods to a boy.

I went to visit my father every afternoon. His voice was sometimes hoarse so that I had to lean close to hear him talk, very often about his boyhood, his mother, and how his father, who was a Protestant, infuriated her by singing Anglican hymns on a Sunday when she was getting the children ready for mass. One day when he was too tired to talk I looked at his chart— now there were two diagrams inside his lungs outlined in red. I came back to the bed and held his hand. It was soft and warm. And I prayed again, making a bargain with God. Telling him I was sorry for thinking I didn't believe in him. I did. Please would He make him better. Please not let him die.

He came home walking more slowly, coughing most of the time and sleeping during the day. 'He'll never work again,' I heard my mother tell her sister. Relations helped, letters came from America and England with money but not sufficient or regular enough to stop us being very poor, and, once my father's stamps were used desperately so. There was relief which could be applied for—it was a humiliating process involving a means test and queuing to receive it if you were approved. My mother balked at the idea. There was also the Society of St Vincent de Paul, which gave food dockets to those they considered worthy—practising Catholics with their homes stripped of all but the bare necessities. My mother said she wouldn't have the St Vincent de Paul cross her door, not if we starved. But she swallowed her pride and applied for relief. And somehow managed to feed and clothe us. In fine weather we wore runners which when the toe went she patched with white rags and pipeclayed over.

There wasn't enough money to buy the leather needed to sole our heavy footwear and in any case my father no longer had the strength to mend shoes. So cardboard was pushed in to cover the holes but the water always seeped in through it. Now my mother walked everywhere and often I walked with her. Into town where bread was a farthing a loaf cheaper. To the Maypole to buy unsalted margarine a bit more palatable than other brands. Ham parings—the scraps from the cooked ham slicing machine; bacon pieces which she sorted carefully—some almost as big as rashers, others minute to be fried crisply; bread fried in grease. And fish—whiting, herrings and mackerel, no more plaice or haddock. Ham bones, pigs' tails and back-bones and once I remember 'elder'—a cow's udder, pale pink and bland tasting but very nourishing, my mother said. Peas and beans and barley she now bought loose, and shell cocoa made from the husk of the cocoa pod which didn't taste at all like cocoa but wasn't unpleasant. I was often not satisfied but never truly hungry. Though now I often wonder if my mother was.

There were other areas, however, where her ingenuity failed. Once a year the list went up on the board for new books. Every text book, pencil, jotter, rubber, pen and nib had to be bought. And as I copied the list I knew I'd never be able to buy them, me and the majority of the class.

And each day we made excuses, 'Sorry Sister I forgot the money. I'll bring it in tomorrow. I left it on the table. My mammy had no change.' Shamefaced, poorly dressed, badly nourished, crippled by our poverty, not one, including me, to stand up and say, 'We've no money. My father's dying. I have eight brothers and sisters. We'll never have the money.'

My father hadn't been a practising Catholic for years. With the realization, though she never admitted it aloud, that he was dying, my mother must have been worried about his salvation. She spoke to the priest and to the nuns, who began visiting my father at home, attempting to bring him back into the fold. The priest, a kindly young, fresh-faced countryman, with infinite patience listened to his criticisms of the Church—its wealth flaunted in the face of the poor, every argument from the Crusades to the Spanish Civil War. And accepted his refusal to take communion. It was physical nourishment he wanted, not spiritual, my father said. Father Phelan did the only thing available to him for relief of hunger—offered my mother tickets for free soup.

'God Bless him,' she said, 'he did what he could,' and she threw the tickets into the fire. 'I wouldn't hurt him by refusing them.'

The nuns sometimes brought half-crowns and a few new laid eggs and promised prayers. And one day in school they called me aside and asked if I would like to go on a holiday. A holiday! I was beside myself with delight. I'd never been on a holiday. And every year watched children who had relations in the country go off to their aunts and grannies and listened to their tales when they came back. The farms, milking cows, feeding chickens, helping with the hay—a holiday was like being a film star—something you dreamed about, but knew in your heart would never come true. And now here I was being offered a holiday. 'I'll have to ask my mammy, Sister.'

'It's at the seaside and tell your mammy it won't cost her a penny.'

Like the day I had been asked about the secondary school, I ran all the way home with my news.

'I can go to Baldoyle for a week, for a holiday. Only I have to let the nun know tomorrow. Can I go, please? Say yes.'

Baldoyle was about fourteen miles from Dublin but I was as excited as if I was about to cross the Atlantic on the *Queen Mary*. Such planning and deliberations as to what I should pack. And then—where would I get an attaché case? Borrow it of course, as with everything out of the ordinary. My aunt ran up a summer dress in a hurry. My mother put new elastic in my knickers and somehow found the money for new socks. But most important of all my father bought me writing paper and envelopes. Probably going without his ounce of tobacco to give me the price of a cardboard flower-decorated case with matching paper and envelopes. I promised to write home every day.

My only regret was that for a week I wouldn't see the boy I was in love with. He was a blonde-haired boy who on Sundays wore velvet short trousers with three pearl buttons on each trouser leg. He was a Protestant, one of only two non-Catholic families living on the road. His father was in constant work and they were very comfortable. Of my love for him he knew nothing. Though sometimes in team games when I was the first one he chose to be on his side I wondered. And when he pulled off my woollen hat or scarf and ran away with it and I chased him and struggled to retrieve it I had hopes that he felt something for me.

In my rearing I had absorbed the knowledge that girls never let their feelings for a boy be known until he had declared his. To do so was to make little of yourself, to throw yourself at him. A boy would have no respect for you if you did that. Just as later my mother warned me that if a boy put his tongue in my mouth he thought nothing of me.

I had a friend to whom I had confessed my love for the blonde-haired boy. And on the night before I went on my holidays I wrote her a letter. Telling her again how much I adored him. And asking for her promise that when I came back she would tell me if he was being attentive to anyone else on the road. And asking for another promise that on her word of honour she wouldn't show the letter to him.

From all around the southside of the city children like myself from homes with idleness or sick parents boarded the bus to take us to Baldoyle. Judging people by the flatness of their accents, as we did in Dublin, I thought some of them were very common. But you could be common and still nice, as a Dubliner I also knew that. All the same with my canvas shoes and my borrowed cardboard suitcase, the bottom barely covered with clothes, I felt very important.

All the way to the coast we sang 'South of the Border Down Mexico Way', 'Old Faithful We Roam the Range Together', 'When Your Round Up Days are Over There'll be Pastures White With Clover', 'Old Faithful Pal of Mine', and when the helpers weren't looking we pelted each other with rolled-up toffee papers.

At the Holiday Home we were greeted by the nuns, mem-
bers of the same Order who taught in my school, and wel-
comed. Told we had to be very good, very clean, very quiet and
no talking after lights out. Everywhere was spotless, the floors
and furniture highly polished and you could smell the sea, or so
I imagined.

For tea we had bread and jam and for supper cocoa, then we
said our prayers, washed our faces and hands and were taken to
our dormatories. Mine was a room with holy pictures and two
rows of iron beds with snowy white counterpanes. The lights
went out and immediately we started whispering to each other,
when no one came to admonish us talking louder, laughing. In a
minute a nun was there telling us how bold we were, how if we
didn't stop at once there'd be no trip to the strand tomorrow.

We had no pranks or midnight feasts as I'd hoped. But in my
memory the sun shone every day. And every day we went to the
beach. A flat sandy one with a calm sea in which we paddled and
tried to swim. And afterwards sat in the sun looking out to sea
and singing 'Red Sails in the Sunset'. Everything about the
holiday was wonderful, even the stewed mince, which I had
never tasted before because my mother maintained that mince
could be anything—minced liver and lights thrown in with the
few bits of meat. I was so happy, so busy and then so tired that I
only wrote one short note home.

Too soon we were on the bus returning to the city. And then
I was on another bus taking me home where everyone was
delighted to see me, kissed and hugged me and exclaimed at
how brown I was. I couldn't wait to go out and play and tell my
friends about my wonderful holiday and catch a glimpse of the
boy who wore velvet trousers on Sundays. He wasn't about.
Neither was my friend. But the other girls were bursting with
news. 'I'd never believe it. Do you know what she did with your
letter—showed it to everyone and to him. Wasn't that terrible.
She's afraid to come out. Afraid of what you'll do to her.'

'Wait'll I get her,' I threatened and made an excuse to go in.
Where I started to cry.

'What ails you?' my mother wanted to know. My father was
concerned and coaxed me to tell him what was the matter with
me. And I sobbed and confessed about the letter. My mother
said, 'That one's a bloody little bitch. I never liked her, she has a
bad mouth. Never trust anyone with thin lips.' And my father
said not to cry, there was nothing really to cry about. But to

remember always that you should never write anything in a letter unless you were very sure that the one you wrote to was someone you could trust. And my mother enlarged on his theme. 'Many a man had lost his life because of writing letters. Letters could be the hanging of you. Once something was down in black and white you couldn't deny it. And if that young wan ever came to the door again she'd run her like a redshank.'

The girl who in my mind had betrayed me avoided me for the next few days. I was very self-conscious with the boy and avoided the games we used to play. He didn't seem to care and then my other friends told me that he was mad about the treacherous one. But it all blew over when quite suddenly his father went to England to work and soon afterwards the family followed, though for a time I hoped that one day I would get a letter from him. I never did.

My father's health got worse. The winter stretched before us making the managing of money harder with firing having to be bought. Sometimes relations would send bags of coal, sometimes a letter would come and tide my mother over the worst. But the respites were only temporary and her struggle to make ends meet went on. She now shopped daily, buying the smallest quantities—penny packets of tea, margarine in two ounces, quarterstone of potatoes, half pound bags of sugar. Never spending anything on herself, always managing the half ounce of tobacco for my father and unheard of extravagance—buying toilet soap. Washing soap, she said, was full of soda and destroyed your skin.

Her dinner was served on a saucer and she filled up on bread. She had frequent bouts of diarrhoea and boils erupted on her neck. Once when she was short taken on a trip into town and went to use a lavatory at the back of a shop, she found a dozen silver packets of spreadable cheese behind the passage door, and was convinced that God had sent her to that very spot. God and luck played such a part in our existence. She was lucky the Christmas Eve when she found thirty shillings on the ground in Moore Street and came home loaded with provisions, a small basket full of chocolates for me and a gift for my brother and sister. Now and then saying that she hoped some poor unfortunate like herself hadn't dropped the money. And when that thought became unbearable, convincing herself that it was some drunken man out to spend more in the pub.

Every day someone we knew died of consumption. Mostly young adults. My mother and her sister talked about the deaths and looked for the reason why young men and women had become infected. 'It was riding racing bikes, all that bending forwards was bad for the lungs. The families had always been delicate. It was too many heavy wettings. Dancing too many nights a week.' They were buried, prayed for and their mothers and fathers pitied. But the living had such a struggle to live and death was so familiar that they appeared to be soon forgotten, except in people's prayers.

Babies got tubercular meningitis and children tuberculosis of the spine and hip—you saw them hunch-backed and lame, and in mass and on the buses there was always the sound of someone coughing. My father coughed constantly. Pennies for the gas had to be put by for when the cough kept him and my mother awake almost all night and she'd go down and make him a cup of hot sweet tea. There were nights, the ones before her weekly payment was due, when there wasn't a penny and the kettle had to be boiled on the fire. I remember being woken one night and going downstairs where she knelt before the fire blowing life into it. And in the night I could appreciate what she was doing but during the days that wasn't so. Hardly one seemed to pass when I wasn't in trouble with her. My greatest fault was back answering, which I did all the time. Questioning and contradicting, refusing to go on errands, to return things to the shops or to borrow anything from a neighbour. She shouted at me and, although I was now taller than her, hit me. I would never cry anymore, standing and trying to stare her out, earning myself another clatter. At night when she thought I was sleeping she came to the room sprinkling holy water, asking God's blessing and protection for us through the night. Pulling the covers round my shoulders and bending to kiss my cheek. Then I'd be truly sorry and resolve never to answer her back again. But the next day at the first order, criticism or suggestion my response was as usual, 'Why should I? I don't care. It's not fair. I won't. No one else has to. Everyone else's mother is different. When I grow up I'll never be like that to my child.'

And I overheard her complain to my aunt and my father, 'I can't get good of her'. They defended me. I was growing up. All children of that age were cheeky. I had a will of my own the same as herself.

It grieved me that my father didn't interfere more when I was in trouble. I wanted him on my side. He must be able to see that everything was my mother's fault. I never meant to be bold—she started it. But more often than not he backed my mother. Afterwards if he and I were alone he would point out that although he knew she was hasty she had a lot to put up with. Things weren't easy for her. I was almost grown up now and should be able to realise that.

His gentle telling off broke my heart for a little while but in the long run made no real difference. I wasn't interested in what my mother had to put up with. Nothing concerned me except myself and the thought of my father dying. It never occurred to me that the aggravation I caused wasn't doing him any good either. I thought only of a time when I wouldn't have him, when he wouldn't be there to answer my questions, to take my part sometimes. I was certain no one loved him like I did. What would I do when he was gone?

***

'Hitler has pulled the wool over Chamberlain's eyes—there's going to be a war,' my father said one night after tea when we were sitting round the fire. My mother was sewing, she was always sewing in the evenings. Mending or darning, refronting a shirt of my father's, turning a collar, sometimes turning a complete garment—remaking it inside out.

My father talked about the Great War—how he had run away from school and joined the Royal Flying Corps. And how his mother had claimed him out because he was under age.

My mother said that she well remembered the last war. 'It only seems like yesterday. Everyone went mad. The fellas were rushing to join up. Hooleys and weddings every night. Married today and off tomorrow. And everywhere you went there were bands playing. The excitement of everything. But that was before the telegrams began coming. Not a day passed without someone you knew getting a telegram and you'd see the families in black all over the city.'

I settled myself comfortably and listened attentively as I always did when my mother talked about long ago. She painted pictures with her telling. I could see the soldiers and the weddings, the band marching.

She recited like a litany the names of men she had known who were killed in the war, Christian names and nicknames.

'Some of the women went to hell with themselves. You'd see them mouldy drunk on the "ring money". Squandering the allowance that they were supposed to be getting a little home together with. For many a poor fella it was as well he never came home to father a bastard.'

It was cosy and safe sitting around the fire listening to my mother talking. My mind so occupied that there was no room in it for thought of my father, now very obviously ill, nor pondering over the war he said was coming.

'Tell us more,' I prompted when she stopped talking. 'Tell me about Nellie and Rosie Donnelly.'

'Ah, poor Nellie and Rosie—two lovely girls—years older than me but I remember them well. Well-reared girls. Two beauties. They had heads of golden hair down to their waists. Pictures they were. God help them they got taken up with soldiers during the war. Officers in the beginning—and the style of them! Off to the races on jaunting cars, done up to the nines. You never saw anything like their hats—gorgeous hats laden down with flowers or wax fruit or birds. But the drink took hold of them and they got a bad name. Everyone in the street talking about them. Anyway they disappeared from the street and no one ever heard a word about them. Their poor mother if she was talking would let on they'd gone to England, but no one believed her.

'Then one day I was over the northside—it was of a Saturday, I can't remember now what took me over there. But anyway didn't I take a wrong turn and wander into a street on the edge of Monto.'

'What was Monto?' I asked. I had a vague idea and hoped my mother, carried away by her reminiscences, might drop a few more hints as to what exactly Monto had been.

'Just a place with public houses and dance halls where soldiers and officers went. It's not there any more. Where was I? Ah yes, so there I was walking down the street. It was a beautiful day with the sun splitting the trees and all the wans out sitting on the doorsteps. Some of them in their bare feet and their blouses open down to their navels showing their camisoles and everything. A brazen-looking lot. I was taking it all in out of the corner of my eye. For you wouldn't have wanted to let on you were watching them. In a minute some of them'd go for you. One of them shouted as I passed "Who are ye looking at?" That's the sort they were. I just kept walking. And the railings out in the front of the street were draped with their washing. Green and blue and red taffeta petticoats, all frills and flounces. And then I saw them, Nellie and Rosie. Not looking like they used to, but all untidy, their feet bare, their golden hair all wild and brassy looking. Them that were the loveliest girls you ever saw, in that place laughing and gossiping with the lowest of the low. I was in a terrible predicament. If I let on not to see them they'd think I was looking down on them, but if I stopped to talk they might be ashamed. For don't forget these were nice, well-reared girls. I couldn't turn back and have the other ones maybe go for me. D'ye see there were bottles on the steps, red biddy, I supppose—they'd have a drink taken. Anyway I kept walking. I could tell they'd spotted me, one of them nudged the other and then they let on to be deep in conversation and never glanced at me as I passed. I never brought up the talk to their mother, God help her.'

She put down her sewing.

'I left the washing out, it might rain, I think I'll bring it in.'

'Don't, not yet,' I protested. 'You haven't finished the story. Tell me the end.'

'About the deadhouse?'

'Yes, that bit, tell me that.'

'That was years after, I was married and had you. I was up in the Union seeing someone waking. There was a good few waking that night, some were coffined and some only on the slabs. And there was this coffin—you could tell it was a pauper's and you'd feel terrible about the corpse with maybe not one to say a prayer for them. So I went over to have a look and who do you think it was only poor Nellie Donnolly. Nellie that used to look like a queen, even the last time I saw her sitting on the doorstep. Nellie that wore the silks and satins and hats weighed down with flowers and fruit, and feathers floating around her and there she was waiting for a pauper's funeral. And I suppose poor Rosie went the same way.'

* * *

The war came but in the beginning made little difference to our lives. People on the road with loyalties to England were in no doubt as to who would win. With the French on their side and the Maginot Line Hitler would be bet into a cocked hat. Republicans said England had met her match, it was the end of her and her Empire. The children took sides reflecting their families' feelings and shouted to each other 'Up the Germans', 'Up the British' in the same way as on Remembrance Day and at Easter we shouted 'Up the Poppies', 'Up the Lilies', the chanting lasting only for the time it took us to think of something else to play. Gas masks were issued. I thought I would suffocate as my head and face were encased and every breath was laden with the smell of rubber. In their cardboard boxes they were placed on top of the wardrobe and eventually thrown out.

In school a teacher pinned a map of the battle area to the wall and with little red flags charted the Axis progress. My father, when I told him, said that some Irish were so anti-British they would support whoever was fighting England. But their German sympathies would be in for a big shock if Ireland was in the North Sea or the Channel.

Men who had been out of work for years went off to England and money-orders came back each week. You couldn't get into the post office and signs of increased prosperity appeared on the road. As the fortunes of others increased so ours declined further.

So badly that once when there wasn't a penny in the house my mother was forced to pawn the Riddle. The Riddle was a tablecloth that had once belonged to my grandmother. From years of laundering and starching it had cracked in the middle so that there were dozens of little holes in the centre. It was used occasionally when someone came to tea, covered by a smaller cloth. But that was seldom nowadays and the cloth lay in its brown-paper laundry wrapping when in desperation my mother decided that, as there was nothing else, she would risk pawning it. She set off to the pawn office where she and the pawnbroker had often exchanged books. If she could get him talking about books, telling him of a very good one she had, *Martin Paz*, maybe he wouldn't spread out the cloth for the usual inspection. Anyway she'd try it. I went with her.

'Two shillings on that Jemmy. Wait'll I tell you about this book. I was going to bring it in to you and left it on the table.

But I'll bring it when I come on Saturday to release the cloth.' She began to tell him the outline of the story. His fingers paused over the twine knot on the paper-wrapped Riddle. 'And the end, you've never read anything like it. I won't spoil it for you, but there's this bit', and she told him the bit.

'Go 'way,' he said. 'That sounds a marvellous story. Don't forget to give me a lend.' He left the knot alone. 'One and six,' he shouted, slinging the parcel to the back of the pawn office, 'and the name is Fox.'

My mother fell about the street laughing when we were far enough away from the pawn.

'Do you know what I'm laughing at?' she asked me.

I said I didn't.

'I'm thinking of when it goes in the pawn and the dealer who buys it thinking she's got a great bargain of a linen tablecloth and when she shakes it out to sell the drop she'll get.'

In high good humour she spent her one and six and said that God was good for tomorrow.

SEVENTEEN

Soon I would be fourteen and leaving school. Already relations were promising that nearer the time they would keep an eye out for a vacancy at the tailoring. My mother had considered Jacobs, as an ex-employee her daughter might be given favourable consideration. It was common knowledge that you had to be walked into a job—it wasn't what you knew but who you knew. But in the long run Jacobs was dismissed. 'The work,' my mother said, 'was killing.' Domestic service, another avenue for fourteen-year-olds looking for employment, was slavery and not if I never worked would she let me do it. Skivvies were worked into the ground for five shillings a week. House-maid's knees before they were twenty and their hands like monkey's paws from all the washing and scrubbing. Please God I'd get into the tailoring—she'd do a novena. Tailoring was a grand job, you were well paid and learnt a trade.

Not only did a relation find me a job but also a coat belonging to her sister in which to start work. I was very sorry to leave school. To know that from the day I left I would be a grown-up—have to go amongst strangers, learn to do something that I might have difficulty learning. Life in school was familiar and safe. I was happy there.

The sight of the coat took my mind off the fact that school was finished and on Monday I was to start work. It was turquoise, a colour I loved and knew suited me. It was cut in a military style, double breasted and made to measure. But the measurements had been someone else's and it was too tight across my chest.

'It doesn't fit me,' I said, and visions of going to work in my old coat plunged me into despair.

'It only wants the buttons shifted, take it off and in two

shakes of a lamb's tail I'll fix it.'

My mother was elated at the prospect of me earning so that her humour was good and nothing too much trouble. The buttons were moved, the fit was good. My skirt and blouse were sponged and pressed, my flat brown lace shoes polished by my father until they gleamed. I had to try everything on and was declared 'lovely'.

But lovely I didn't think I was or ever would be. Long sessions of studying myself at my aunt's triple-mirrored dressing-table had convinced me of this. A beautiful coat couldn't trans-form me. Couldn't alter my straight bobbed brown hair or grow out my fringe, make my pimples disappear. Everything about me was wrong. My eyes too small, my nose too big. I hated myself, hated my face.

But hate it or not I wasn't likely to get another before morning, so I scrubbed it and plastered my forehead and chin with sulphur ointment—the supposed cure for pimples. In the morning my mood had swung high and the thought of wearing the new coat, going into town with my mother and even starting work, got me out of bed, washed and dressed and in a state of nervous excitement.

My father kissed me and wished me good luck. Then in honour of the special occasion my mother and I squandered money on the bus-fares into town.

'You'll get the job,' she assured me as we walked down the narrow street to the factory. 'Anyone can see that you're a lovely intelligent girl.'

Wearing her one and only pair of high-heeled shoes, her dark coat and with not a hair out of place beneath her home-dyed, retrimmed dark straw hat she was the picture of confidence. Beside her I felt awkward, aware of how big my feet were compared with hers, how flat-footed I must appear by the side of her little high-instepped, daintily shod feet.

My mother knocked on one of the two doors at the top of the landing and, when someone came, gave her name and that of the relation who had spoken for me and asked to see the manager. After a few minutes a man about my father's age, a Jewish man with an English accent, came out to see us and again my mother gave her own and her relation's name. The man, who was the manager, said that yes, there was a vacancy, and that I could start straightaway. He was sure that if I worked like my cousin I'd get on. My mother thanked him and handed me the packet of sandwiches she had brought in case I was started immediately.

The manager asked me my name and I gave him the one that was on my birth certificate. 'But everyone calls me ...' and I told him what everyone called me. I followed him into the factory. There were so many people and so much noise. Men and women stopped what they were doing for a minute to look at the new girl. Mr Fisher beckoned a girl about my own age who left a table on which coats were piled up and came to him. 'Show her where to hang her coat and then she's to sit with you. Show her what to do.'

Back at the table she pointed to the coats, explaining 'You have to pull out all the bastings, every single bit of white thread. You'll have to get a bodkin, they sell them round the corner, you can buy one at dinnertime.'

'Is that all I'll have to do, pull out the threads?'

'You're a runner as well.'

'A runner?'

'Do the messages. Needles and thread and drinks of water for the oul' wans, and take things to the cutting room. It's easy. Wait'll I show you how to rip out the bastings. Here, have a lend of this scissors.'

At dinnertime my relation introduced me to the other women. Many of them knew my mother and my aunt and some knew my father by sight. I felt very at home. After eating the sandwiches I went with my new friend to buy the white bone bodkin.

My father was eager to hear all about my first day. Had I liked it? Was the work difficult? Was the manager nice—the other people?

'I loved it. It was easy and everyone was grand. And the manager calls me Nella.'

My mother had made a stew. My portion had simmered for hours so that the meat was very tender and the gravy so thickened it had almost caught—the way I liked it. I was ravenous.

'We were right weren't we?' my mother said as she wet the tea. 'God spoke before that bloody little quack in the Meath. You lived to see her go to work and you'll live to see them all do the same, please God.'

By the end of the week I was used to the noise of the power-driven industrial sewing-machines and the variety of them. Ones with enormous needles and curved needles and the king of them all, the Reece, placed higher than the others on the bench—a clattering, clacking machine which cut and worked buttonholes, its operator almost venerated for her skill. The cheaper clothing was made by machine from start to finish. Piece-workers fed side seams, sleeves, linings, pockets and collars through the machines, stopping only when satisfied they were making up their wages, then entering the amount of work in little red notebooks, having the entry checked, and going down to the lavatory for a quick smoke.

Once the factory had been the University's Anatomy Department. Older women who had worked in the factory since its beginning told stories of gruesome things they found in jars left behind by the anatomists. I never doubted them and on my trips to the cellars for buckets of turf dreaded what I might unearth as I rooted in the piles of sods, though the only things I ever disturbed were rats which scurried away.

As a newcomer I had practical jokes played on me. I fell for the first one. A man who operated a Hoffman steam-press sent me to the cutting room for a bucket of steam. To the great amusement of everyone I went and asked for it. But the laughter was good-natured so I didn't feel a fool. And before very long I was playing my own more cruel practical jokes. Occasionally dropping salt into the water for the oul' wans and, convulsed by the expressions on their faces, swearing, 'Honest to God Lizzie I didn't do it on purpose. The salt must've been in the cup. Will I get you another one?'

At the end of the week I proudly brought home my first pay packet—one ten shilling note, one shilling and a sixpence.

'May God bless you,' my mother said fondling the note. 'Have the one and six for yourself.'

My father said he was very proud of me.

One of my mother's economies since my father had stopped working was to use salt instead of toothpaste. Out of my pocket money I bought a large tube of Colgate and probably spent the remainder on sweets and chocolates.

In the factory we were allowed to sing but officially not supposed to talk. Singing I suppose helped production, there was the rhythm and you could sing and sew, sing and press, sing and pull bastings. Talking required eye contact, gestures. The ban on talking wasn't rigorously enforced or obeyed unless a rush order was going through or the 'oul' man' was on the floor. Everyone except the older employees who had worked with him before he started his own business was afraid of the 'oul' man'. Though even those afraid of him admitted that he was a fair man, paid the top rates and was the best tailor in Dublin.

He came to the floor only on occasions: if a customer had complained about a garment, if an unusual one was to be made or when an order had been delayed. Then the one responsible for the delay or poor workmanship was roared at. The roaring was terrifying though hardly a word of it was intelligible for, great though his tailoring might be, his command of English deserted him in a rage.

Once there was a terrible scene. Pocket flaps from a special order had been lost and there wasn't enough of the expensive cloth to cut more. The cutters swore the flaps had been sent up to the workroom, the machinist that she had never laid eyes on them. Mr Fisher, who was production as well as general manager, bore the brunt of the oul' man's anger. More from habit than piety or belief I said to him that I would say a prayer to St Antony. 'He's good at finding things,' I added. And lo and behold the missing flaps were found on the stairs between the cutting and machine room. Ever after when anything important was lost Mr Fisher would say, 'Nella, a prayer to your private detective, please.' Mr Fisher was a very nice kind man. When he discovered that I liked reading he lent me books.

There were many nice men working in the factory. One who looked like the holy pictures of Our Lord, with a golden ginger beard and hair of the same colour receding on a high noble forehead. His English was accented and when he stood to talk to you he held his hands one clasped in the other and rocked gently back and forwards. He was softly spoken and very courteous, thanking you profusely when you brought a message. But my favourite man was a tailor called Sean who stitched all day cross-legged on the table. He was stout and red-faced, unmistakably Irish. Behind his rimless glasses his eyes smiled, and once he told me how when he was a journeyman tailor he had worked his way to Rio de Janeiro and described his delight and astonishment on the morning he docked and saw the beautiful harbour for the first time.

There were also lovely girls and women. Some did wonders for my morale, so that I came to realize that straight hair, a fringe and pimples weren't the disfiguration I considered them. Others talked to me about operas they had seen or plays they went to. And one very beautiful girl a little older than myself told me the story of *Hamlet* and taught me the soliloquy; from her I learned that Julius Caesar was not the only Roman Emperor—there was also Tiberius who lived on the Isle of Capri.

So many things I learned as I brought needles and thread and drinks of water. Such endless kindness and affection I had showered on me.

With so much in my favour and the extra privileges granted by my mother—permission to go to the pictures occasionally after work, not asked any more to do messages and the promise of being allowed to go to a dance soon—she and I were getting on well. Until the coat.

Opera, the theatre and Roman Emperors were discussed in work but only seldom—style was the main topic of conversation: what was the latest in clothes, hair, shoes, everything you wore; navy or black or chalk-striped tailor-made suits, crêpe-de-Chine and georgette blouses, pale chamois leather gloves, handbags to match or contrast with a blouse or shoes, where you could buy real silk stockings. Fashions seen in films and in the big shops in town were hankered after. I listened to the descriptions, looked at clothes brought in to be displayed by their owners and longed to be able to have something new.

There were money-clubs run in work to make the buying of the latest fashions easier. A group of people agreed to pay a certain sum each week, and entered a draw. The result decided which week they would take the proceeds of the club. You might be lucky and pick number one and have the money immediately, or with luck against you you picked the last number. And I wanted the coat now. I knew which one. Every day at lunch time I went to look at it. It was pure wool, heliotrope and the last word in style. It cost forty-nine and eleven.

I talked about it to my relation, showed it to her. She said it was gorgeous, it would suit me.

'You could get it on a docket—ask your mammy.'

The docket granted you instant credit and made half-a-crown in the pound for the woman who organized them. I thought about the coat morning, noon and night, hurrying to the shop with my breath in my fist, fearful that the coat would be gone. But it was still there, the centre of the window display.

'Ask your mammy,' my relation urged again.

I asked my mammy politely and reasonably. And politely and reasonably she refused.

'Why can't I? It's not fair. I'm working. Everyone else gets new clothes.'

'You're not everybody. Shut up about it and eat your dinner.'

I shut up and thought instead about the coat. My need of it, my hunger for it. How once I had it I could take part in the talk of clothes. Describe it the way the others described their purchases. I needed it in the same way I needed food. As if from a long way off, so far away that it didn't concern me, a voice was saying, 'God knows I wouldn't begrudge you the coat. With a heart and a half if I could afford it you'd have it. But I can't— your ten shillings is the rent and half a crown to start me through the week.' It was as if I had suddenly developed a hearing defect so that I heard sounds of words but not their meaning. And while the distorted sounds continued I made up my mind—I was having the coat.

Always on pay-day I brought my mother my unopened pay packet, but not this Friday. Already I had asked Mr Fisher if I could be let off ten minutes early. Telling him a lie—I had a message to collect from the chemist—medicine for my father. The transaction was completed with the woman who 'ran the dockets'. Never doubting that I had my mother's permission, on the receipt of half-a-crown she gave me the means to buy the coat.

I ran all the way to the shop, praying they wouldn't for some unlikely reason have closed early. They were open and the coat still there and in my size. I put it on, caressing the soft wool of it, turned up the collar and tied the belt, put my hands in my pockets and stood before the glass. It was beautiful. I was made beautiful by it. 'Yes,' I said. 'Yes I'll take it, please.'

I held the parcel close to me on the way home, but carefully close, like a baby or a kitten, securely without squashing. I went in through the back door, leaving the parcel in the porch, not daring to present the coat straight away. First I'd see what reception the opened pay packet got.

'All silver,' she said weighing the packet in her hand not yet noticing the open flap. She was all smiles—I was home with my wages, the place was set for dinner, everything was lovely, as it should be on pay-day. Then her smile went. 'Com'ere,' she said, 'what's this—the packet's open, what happened?' She was very generous. I could have lied and said there had been a collection—a girl had lost her wages, we made it up; someone's mother, brother or father died, we bought a wreath. If I'd put a sixpence of hers and sixpence of mine she wouldn't have objected.

She poured the coins into her hand. Before she counted or said anything else, defiantly I said, 'I opened it to pay the docket money.'

'What docket money, what are you talking about?'

'I bought a coat. Ah wait Mammy, wait'll you see it, it's lovely. Wait'll I show it to you.' I ran out to the porch and back again pulling out the coat, tearing the paper in my nervousness. 'Look at it. Look, isn't it lovely?' I didn't know what she would do. Scream, pounce on me, hit me. I was keyed up for any or all of these responses, prepared to put up with them for the sake of the coat.

Her silence frightened me far more than any threat or scream. It seemed to last forever, then she said. 'If I wasn't so stupefied with what you've done I'd reef it off you and back the fire with it. I can't believe it! I can't credit it! Knowing my straits you'd do that. Leave me short of the rent or short of the half-crown I depend on for the next week's food. I can run the rent in arrears but you can't eat in arrears. I'm choked. May God forgive you—a child to do that on her mother—God forgive you.'

Before her stricken, shocked face I was devastated. She seldom cried but did then.

'Oh I'm sorry Mammy, I'm terrible sorry. Listen—I let on to the woman you said I could have it. I'll tell her the truth. It'll be all right and they'll take back the coat. I'll bring it back on Monday.'

I was crying, trying to make amends.

'And have yourself branded as a liar—you'll do no such thing. Besides you can't—the coat's been bought—the docket spent—it'll have to be paid for. But I'll never forgive you, never.'

Later in the same evening my father broke my heart when he told me how disappointed he was in me. He knew, he said, how important new clothes were to people at my age. But I was old enough and sensible enough to know the way things were. To realize how my wages were my mother's mainstay. I had been very selfish.

Right then I'd have done anything to undo what I had done. I offered to go without my one and six but my mother said no, for then I'd have no bus-fare if the weather was bad and she wouldn't want me to be a beggar in work, not able to buy a penny cake if the others were buying cakes, or contribute to someone collecting.

I don't know how she managed to make up for the lost half-crowns, but we were fed and the rent and society money paid; probably she ate less herself. She was kind and generous but had a long memory and for years afterwards in rows would remind me of what I had done on her when she was in serious want.

EIGHTEEN

I could have been a runner forever once I discovered there was more to it than fetching needles, thread and drinks of water. There were messages, unofficial ones, instructions whispered to you by machinists or tailors, threepenny bits and sixpences pressed into your hand for yourself; 'two ounces of cheese, two cakes from Roberts, chips on Friday, twenty Woodbines, twenty Sweet Afton, go down the back stairs when Mr Fisher's not looking. If he asks we'll let on you're in the lavatory.' And official messages—across the river to another factory to borrow shoulder pads, take letters, bank private savings, buy Bridge Rolls. I could have been a runner forever.

Between the factory and the Liffey I wove in and out of narrow streets: old cobbled streets with intriguing names, Crown Alley, Merchant's Arch, Temple Bar, Fishamble Street. Streets lined with tall houses, their bottom floors little shops, watchmakers, printers, shops that sold only buttons. Lanes and alleys within a stone's throw of the Ha'penny Bridge on which I stood, looking up and down the quays at the other bridges, seagulls, crowds passing; and smelled the sea when the tide was coming in.

And not too far away—often part of my run—Grafton Street and College Green. Crowded with beautiful women in gorgeous clothes, and students from Trinity who seemed to tower above everyone else. Grafton Street smelled of roasting coffee beans, the smell wafted from the ever-opening doors of Bewley's, Roberts and Mitchells. And such cakes there were in the windows! Cakes covered in flaked chocolate, topped with toasted almonds, fruit cakes and buns from which plump sultanas and raisins peeped. Cakes showered with coconut, little cakes made to look like miniature cauliflowers, their outer casing pale green marzipan, the centre flowers whipped cream.

Up the street I went, looking at confectionery and sweets in

Lemons, clothes and furs in Brown Thomas's, weird-shaped glass bottles and surgical aids in the chemist that used to stock the artificial snow which eased my father's throat; at the dealers' baskets overflowing with brilliant coloured flowers. Gazing into windows of shops that sold antiques, gleaming furniture and silver—and the shop that sold pictures. And at the top of the street I could see St Stephen's Green and was tempted. But runners were timed, if only loosely, and the clock near the corner told me it was time to go back.

The days flew. Away from the house my mind was constantly occupied—rediscovering the city, watching the process of tailoring, the bundles of pieces that came up from the cutting room being transformed into suits and overcoats, the skill of tailors and tailoresses. Men who with hundreds and hundreds of stitches bonded canvas to cloth in a way which rolled a collar. Men who with canvas and wadding layered between lining and cloth corrected the dropped shoulders, hollow backs and other physical defects of customers. Pressers who stretched or shrunk cloth as necessary and elderly craftswomen who with thick silken thread embroidered perfect buttonholes.

And there was dancing too. In a wide corridor at lunchtime girls who danced every night demonstrated the latest quicksteps, foxtrots and tangos. Fishtailing while the onlookers provided the music, tangoing to our chorus of 'Tangerine', heads at right angles, bodies bent down, down, righting themselves and gliding on. We all had a turn. Practised dancers taking the uninitiated round. Starting them on slow waltzes. The girl who pulled out bastings with me jitterbugged and I envied her ability to perform with apparent ease the wild, fast steps, kicks, twists and turns. She gave me endless lessons, assuring me it was easy, I'd pick it up.

But working and running and dancing finished and it was time to go home. As soon as I entered and smelt the smell of burning metal I knew it was one of my father's bad days. That he was in bed and that my mother had carried from the front-room fire a shovelful of burning coals to the grate in his bedroom. I'd go up and see him. Sometimes he was dozing, sometimes reading the paper, following the war. And his beautiful face that had become so thin smiled at me and I was overwhelmed with love and sadness. And resentment flared in me. It wasn't fair. Why him? Why did he have to lie in bed, not able to go to work. When we first moved to the house he was one of the few men working. Now almost everyone had a job, was in England working. It wasn't fair. It was God's fault. And my mother's. She should have made him go to a sanatorium. I would have had it been my husband. He might have got better. I'd have made him go. I wouldn't have cared about what the neighbours thought. She didn't love him. Not like I did. She couldn't. If she did she'd be broken-hearted. How could she go round singing, talking and laughing as if nothing was happening? Nobody loved him like me. When he died so would I.

And after such a night I went off blithely to my work and for eight hours thought of neither mother nor father.

The priest and nuns continued to visit and still my father refused the sacraments. My mother was praying that he would relent. Sometimes she tried to talk to me, but I didn't want to hear her mention the word die. I could think about it, but to mention it out loud was to bring it nearer, to let it in the door. It entered my mind to cross-hackle her. Say, 'How can he die if there is nothing wrong with him?' It would have given me some satisfaction to discomfort her, but I wouldn't utter that word.

One day towards the end of the summer I came home and found my mother in a delighted humour.

'Thanks be to God,' she said, 'my prayers were answered. He received this morning and do you know he looks better all ready.'

The part of me that wanted to believe in God was delighted too. For if there was a heaven, and if he had to die, I wanted my father to go there. And yet I was afraid in case he was afraid and that was why he had taken communion. I went into the back garden to see him. He was sitting on the granite step that never made a rockery. And he did look better, or so I thought, and he didn't seem afraid of anything. Only worried that the war wasn't going as well as he wished it. He whispered a lot now, his hair cut very short like the crew-cuts that were to come years later.

When he had had it cut that way my mother was annoyed. 'You've destroyed your lovely hair,' she said. 'It looks a show.'

And he had replied, 'I couldn't bear the weight of it—it made me too hot.'

I sat on the step and we talked. He promised again that when he was well and working we'd go to England. Only we might have to wait until after the war.

He asked me about work and I told how the day had gone. That soon I might be put on a machine. That women working in the factory said you weren't a real machinist until you 'got the needle'. He asked what that meant and I explained. If you were machining very fast sometimes the needle went through your nail and right into your finger. I'd seen it happen. It would be very sore especially when you had to raise the needle from your finger.

'Getting the needle', he said, 'has nothing to do with being a good machinist—it's carelessness. If you go on a machine use it properly. And don't believe everything the women tell you. Learn to think for yourself.'

'Oh I do,' I assured him. 'Since you told me holy water didn't make the public cup safe to drink from in chapel I haven't touched it—not even when other girls from work are there and say, "You can't catch anything from it—it's holy." Mr Fisher says that maybe later on he'll put me in the Reception Office.'

'Would you like that?'

'I'd love it. Only I'd have to go to night school and learn typing and shorthand. Maybe I wouldn't be able to understand them.'

'You would. You could learn anything, do anything, if you wanted to.'

I believed it because he said it.

There were things about work I didn't tell him. That a young man who had been off sick was dead—a young girl, a machinist, was going into a sanatorium. The dead boy and the girl had tuberculosis. Nearly everyone I knew had someone in their family with tuberculosis—some had several, mothers and fathers, brothers and sisters.

The weeds grew high where the potato and cabbage used to be. Looking around at them my father said that next year he would do a good job on the garden. Maybe in a day or two he would tidy it up, make a bonfire. My mother called through the kitchen window, 'Your dinner is on the table.'

'Don't let it go cold,' my father said.

'Aren't you coming in?'

'I'll stay here for a while—it's a nice evening. Soon they'll be getting dark.'

Sometimes while I worked or sat at lunchtime in a group listening to the talk of clothes, dances or the progress of a romance I felt restless inside myself. Dissatisfied without knowing why. Seeing the factory as if for the first time, the bare discoloured walls, the grimy windows, the skylight which stretched from one end of the room to the other festooned with cobwebs. The uncovered floorboards, grey with age and dirt, covered with cloth clippings and snarls of thread. The woman who made the tea and cleaned the factory sweeping the floor, shaking water from a milk bottle to damp down the dust which formed into grey globules and moved before the broom. Although edgy and restless, I didn't understand that the surroundings depressed me; that being confined to the factory endlessly ripping out white threads, slinging the garment to the pressers, the table piling up again with more suits, more overcoats, didn't satisfy or stimulate me. And so I'd sit until someone said, 'What's the matter with you, you have a face like a fiddle on you.'

And I'd smile, shrug and say, 'Nothing, I was just thinking'.

Sometimes I'd have a lovely surprise. I'd be told I was wanted downstairs, and downstairs would be my aunt. 'I was in town,' she'd say, 'and thought you'd like this for your lunch.' Always it was something delicious, two slices of ham or roast pork, a cake, fruit. Something she knew I loved. On the days she didn't come I put my packet of bread on top of the pot-bellied stove ten minutes before lunchtime with the other young girls. When you could smell the paper beginning to singe your lunch was done. The bread crisped but not coloured and the butter or margarine melting and golden yellow.

The summer was dying, the mornings and evenings cold, the buildings etched sharply against the sky. I ran my errands more quickly, not lingering so long on the Ha'penny Bridge, and the smell of roasting coffee and cakes was more tantalizing. To save money, and probably to delay my return to the house, I often walked home. Now my father seldom left his bed. One night when I came in my mother told me that the priest and nuns had called that day and talked to her about my father going into the Hospice for the Dying.

'There's many a one,' she said, 'that went in and lived to come out. I knew plenty. The priest broached the subject to him and he's going to think about it.'

I don't know what I thought or felt. Maybe an acceptance of what was to come was in me. But on the first night I went to see my father in the hospice it was different. It was autumn and the leaves were falling as I walked under the big metal arch. Along the drive where I had pushed my sister's pram long ago the lamps had a yellow haze about them. I wanted to be sick when the big many-windowed building came in sight. There were many lighted windows and behind one of them was my father's ward. Filled with dying people. People in their last agony, moaning and writhing, screaming perhaps. I was preparing myself for something so horrendous that I longed to collapse, never reach the door.

Full of terror and apprehension, I forced myself to walk on, walk in, and it was like nothing I had imagined. It was very warm inside the hall, very clean and there were lots of statues and holy pictures and nuns moving about briskly but noiselessly except for a swish of their robes. I found the ward—a long narrow room. It was warm in there as well with more religious objects and flowers and visitors grouped round beds talking and laughing. Then I saw my father and he was waving to me. I hurried to his bed, all my fears banished at the sight of him. He looked so well. He was smiling and holding my hand and I bent to kiss his cheek. It was so normal—talking about my work and the war. Telling me my mother had been in in the afternoon. I squirted soda from a syphon a man he used to work with had brought him. He said it was so hot in the ward he was thirsty all the time.

'And your throat?' I asked.

The nun, he said, was giving him gargles. But the best thing was not to talk too much, she had advised him. I was so relieved, so happy—he looked as if nothing ailed him. I said I'd come again the next night. And before I left he gave me half a crown for my mother. The man who had brought him the syphon had slipped him the money.

People were always slipping money to someone less well off. Slipping shillings into hands, little parcels of food into shopping bags. Making excuses about gifts they brought. 'I made a mistake and bought too many eggs, I hope you won't be offended with a few.' Or if the gift was clothes, 'My young wan has had a stretch. This won't go near her. There isn't a brack on it, it's a sin to throw it out.' The gracious giving went on all over the city, all over the country. Money and food, clothes and time. Advice and consolation. People to sit with the dying, to sit all night with the bereaved, to go with you to see the doctor, to answer a summons, to lend a pledge for the pawn. A woman on the estate kept 'the dead bundle'—bed linen, candlesticks and a crucifix to lend to those who hadn't the means to wake their dead with dignity, asking only that the linen should be laundered on return.

It had to be that way. State help was non-existent. A minimum relief system and charity doled out at the discretion of those dispensing it. Cold charity too crushing for anyone with pride. Means and morals tested charity.

NINETEEN

Even though my father seemed better than he had been for a long time—his eyes bright and his cheeks flushed, which I interpreted as a return to health, not the fever which accompanied TB, and in spite of his delight at seeing me, his eagerness to hear my news and tell me his, now mostly in a whisper, I came to dread the visiting. Coming in from the cold fresh night the heat in the hospice was overpowering and there was a smell to which I couldn't put a name but guessed that it was compounded of so many sick and dying people gathered in the same place. I was frightened and nauseated by it so that when I got home I had no appetite for the food waiting for me. My picking at it and pushing it about the plate caused rows.

'Why aren't you eating your dinner?'

'I'm not hungry.'

'You must be hungry—you've had nothing substantial in your stomach since morning. Eat it or you'll destroy your health.'

I wasn't interested in my health and couldn't understand that my mother was. Not until many years later was I to know her constant fear that we might become infected with TB. I wouldn't eat and with my father not there to act as a go-between the rows escalated. I excelled myself in contradicting, criticizing and condemning her for not visiting him in the evenings. And she defended herself.

'I go every afternoon. Someone has to be here at night to mind the others and have a bit of dinner ready for you.'

I wasn't impressed. Neither was I impressed when she repeated to me, to her relations and friends why my father had gone into the hospice.

'He did it for me and the children. Do you know what he said, God help him? He said, "I've been thinking it over and I'll go in for a while. You're run off your feet up and down the stairs night and day and dragged out of your sleep with me coughing. And the bit of money will go further without me to feed." There's a man for you—to put everyone of us before himself.'

I didn't believe her. She was glad he was in there. Glad she could sleep through the night. I didn't believe he had said any of those things. How could he? How could anyone voluntarily go into the Hospice for the Dying? She was making everything up. She must have encouraged him, let him know she found him a burden, that we'd be better off not having to feed him. I kept these thoughts to myself. Afraid perhaps of openly accusing her, or perhaps I had sufficient grace and feeling not to make such callous accusations. I can never be sure why—only thankful that I never voiced them.

The dinner would be thrown out and then she'd coax me to have an egg done the way I loved eggs if I wasn't well—the way she prepared eggs for babies—softly boiled and beaten in a cup with breadcrumbs, pepper and salt and a nob of butter. Hunger always got the better of me and I'd have the egg, two if she had them. My mood would improve and the evening pass.

Then two things happened which took the edge off my fear of visiting the hospice. I had two relations working with me, the one who had got me the job and her younger sister in whose coat I had started work. One night she suggested that she would walk home with me and come to visit my father. There was only a little difference in our ages and we got on well.

Her humour was quick and caustic and she had a fund of anecdotes to which I listened on our walk to the hospice. 'Do you see that wan?' she'd say as we passed and saluted someone. 'Well wait'll I tell you.' Then would follow a tale, sometimes tragic, sometimes hilarious, often scandalous. I laughed, was astounded, saddened or horrified. My mind had no time to dwell on fear and my stomach wasn't knotted in apprehension. And when we came across an officious nurse or a nun with quick retorts she made short work of them.

When visiting was over she encouraged me greatly as to my father's health. Wrinkling her small pretty face into a smile she'd say, 'That fella's having you all on. Did you look at him—he's thriving. I'm telling you he knows when he's well off. Stall-fed and the nuns dancing attendance on him! No wonder he likes it. They'll throw him out of here before long. Keeping a bed under false pretences.'

I'd listen to every word and take hope. Not understanding it was her way of trying to help me. Not realizing for another forty years, when she and I went to visit someone else dying in the hospice, that she had been as terrified as I was when as two young girls we had visited my father. Not until now as a middle-aged woman she squeezed my hand and said, 'This place turns my insides to water,' and had to run and find a lavatory.

The other event that lightened my life at this time when my father was dying was my promotion to the Reception Office. I was thrilled. My mother and father were delighted. My father wanted to know if I would get a rise and had my status been altered. I didn't know. I hadn't asked.

'Well find out,' he advised. 'Working in the office you may not have the union's protection, such as it is. Find out where you stand.'

I said 'yes' but had no intention of doing so. It didn't matter to me whether I was in the union or not. I was in the office and full of my own importance. Entering orders in ledgers, checking bales of materials, making out dockets with the customers' measurements and physical shortcomings called out by the old man. There were no needles and threads or drinks of water to fetch but still the errands in between my clerical work which gave me the run of my beautiful city.

Suits and coats were sometimes brought back for alterations. One of my duties was to search the pockets before garments went up to the workroom in case any valuables had been left in them. I often imagined finding a wallet or important document and being complimented for my diligence. One day I did find something. I had no idea what it was. It was reddish in colour and resembled a peculiar-shaped balloon. I felt it and pulled it but couldn't make head or tail of it. Then as was usual with me I decided to smell it and was about to lift it to my nose when the woman who was in charge of the reception came in.

'What's that? What are you doing?'

'I found it in the justice's pocket. I don't know what it is,' I said, bending my head towards it. She hit it out of my hand and with her foot kicked it towards the door.

'Go and get the brush and dust-pan,' she ordered 'and then wash your hands.'

'But why—what is it?'

'Just do what you're told and don't ask questions.'

I was a bit scared of her so didn't persist. At dinner time I asked the girl I used to pull bastings with if she knew what it was. I described it as well as I could. She didn't know either and we decided that my boss was a bit of a crank.

Christmas was coming and the shops were full of lovely things—especially the chemists. I hoped someone would buy me a bottle of scent for Christmas. A little blue bottle of Evening in Paris. My aunt gave my mother the makings of her Christmas pudding and promised her a half of ham. I helped my mother chop the candied peel and when she wasn't looking ate sultanas and raisins and even picked at the suet—I liked raw suet. The pudding was boiled for hours then removed from its cloth and a new one was wrapped round it before it was hung in the pantry. My mother said it would be a beauty and that no one could touch her when it came to making a plum pudding.

A couple of weeks before Christmas she was notified by the Customs that a parcel had arrived from America—there was duty to be paid on it. She had no money to pay the duty and for ages we wondered what marvellous things we had lost.

As Christmas came nearer my mother kept hoping that my father could come home, if only for a holiday.

'It won't be the same without him. Tomorrow when I go in I'll ask the nun. I could bring down a single bed and I'll borry the money for a taxi. I'm sure she won't refuse. Say a prayer now when you go to bed that he'll be well enough.'

The nun said 'no' and explained that he wasn't well enough to be moved. My mother didn't believe her.

'You know what it is—they don't like anything upsetting their routine. It discommodes them discharging and then having to readmit people.'

We believed my mother and agreed that nuns could be very unfeeling, for as far as we could see my father looked grand.

I got the little blue bottle of Evening in Paris from a cousin and a pair of gloves to match my coat. They were heliotrope on one side and pale lemon on the other and were embroidered with flowers of both colours. My father had sent money given to him by visitors and my mother bought a small gift for each of us. Apart from the half of ham and plum pudding she didn't have a present from anyone.

I suppose we all went to visit my father on Christmas after-noon, but I only remember being there with my aunt. All the patients had new bedjackets in a shade of green that wasn't very attractive. The ward was hung with paper chains and bells and everything was very festive. The visiting hour was extended and half way through a nun brought in a wind-up gramophone. Visitors and patients sang along with the music. Then an old-fashioned waltz was put on. A couple of women got up.

'Get up and we'll dance,' my aunt said.

'I don't know how—only the slow waltz.'

'Now's your chance to learn—there's no time like the present.'

'Do,' my father said.

So up I got, towering above my dainty little aunt in her high-heeled size three-and-a-half shoes. She took the lead and guided me round and round, counting out the time. And up and down the ward we waltzed past the propped-up patients who watched and smiled and nodded their heads in time to the music. And my father was smiling as I floated by his bed and when the dance was over he told me how well I had done. And my aunt said I was as light as a feather and would make a great dancer.

My father saw two white doves on the windowsill facing his bed. He told my mother that it was a funny thing because it was in the middle of the night yet he could see them plainly. Then the doves flew away and his mother was there standing by the window—only her face kept changing. One minute it was his mother and the next the Blessed Virgin. When my mother related the stories to her sister my aunt said he must have been dreaming.

'All the same I don't like it—you know what they say. Before you die you see your mother.'

'Don't pay any attention to your mother,' my aunt said to me when I started to cry. 'The weather's taken a turn for the worse since Christmas and your father caught a cold. He was feverish, a bit delirious. You imagine all sorts of things and have strange dreams in a fever. You said yourself he was grand when you saw him tonight.'

'Yes,' I said, 'he was grand. Even his sore throat was better.' And then I remembered something else, something that made me believe what my aunt was saying.

'He wants you,' I said to my mother, 'to bring in a shirt and socks for him. The nun asked for them.'

'A shirt and socks—why didn't you tell me that before? Are

you sure that's all?'

I told my mother that was all and she puzzled her brains—talking out loud wondering what the nun wanted a shirt and socks for. Then convinced herself that either I only got half of the message or had forgotten. The nun must have asked for his trousers. That was it—there was an improvement. They were letting him up. She'd bring in his trousers tomorrow.

The clothes weren't mentioned again. But from that day on my mother was there at the hospice every evening when I came home from work, having arranged for someone to mind the children. In a way I regretted this for it meant less time for me with my father. She sat close to him and held his hand and talked and talked so that I couldn't get a word in edgeways. Since my mother started visiting in the evenings my cousin had stopped coming and although I had my mother's company on the way home I had to walk on my own to the hospice. Always when we were going home my mother talked about how when she was a little girl she had gone to the school in the hospice grounds. And that when she was dying it was in the hospice she wanted to die. I thought she was mad.

On the morning I was sent for to the General Office, thoughts of my father were far from my mind. The previous night he had seemed better than I remembered for a long time. The hoarseness had left his voice and for a part of the visit he sat without using his bed rest. He had had a letter that week from his brother in America and showed me a reply he was writing. The first paragraph was full of incredulity that he who had been so fit could now be laid so low. He kept reminding his brother of how strong and agile he had been. Asking him if he remembered such and such a thing involving feats of strength they had done as boys and young men.

'Sometimes,' he wrote, 'I think I'm still dreaming when I wake up and find myself here in bed.'

The letter then went on about Pearl Harbour. I skipped that part but let on to read it.

'I'll finish it tomorrow,' he said when I handed it back.

We kissed him.

'He looks grand,' my mother said as we stopped by the door to look back. He was waving to us, sitting up wearing his green bed jacket.

I ran up to the General Office and went in. My face lighting up as I saw another relation of mine, one I was very fond of but didn't see often as she worked in another part of the city. Only afterwards I realized that everyone in the office had been very quiet when I came in. 'Your daddy died this morning,' my cousin said, putting her arms around me. I was the centre of attention and aware of it, my mind taking everything in. People going away to fetch my coat and bag. My daddy was dead, suits waiting to be wrapped were left on the counter, the secretary was standing by her door looking solemn. My cousin was crying silently, tears falling down her face as she helped me put on my coat. Mr Fisher came in and asked if I had money for the bus. And then the others spoke. They were all very sorry. He's dead and I'll never see him again, I thought, as we walked down the stairs. And as we walked to the bus stop I kept seeing people laughing, hurrying, eating in cafés and none of them knew my father was dead.

'Three o'clock this morning he died. I woke and looked at the clock—it was exactly three o'clock. The nun said he died calling my name,' my mother said. She began to cry. 'If only I'd known it was his last night on earth I wouldn't have left his side.'

The house was full of people coming and going, offering their sympathy. A relation said wasn't it a funny thing—she woke in the night and heard a crash and when she got up to look a picture had fallen from the wall and the clock downstairs was striking three. 'But I didn't give him a thought, Lord have mercy on him, he was so well lately.'

Another one said, 'That was the change before death—they seem to be on the mend and then ...'

'I knew it but wouldn't let myself believe it,' my mother said. 'Do you remember when the nun asked for a shirt and socks? And God help me didn't I think there was an improvement and they were letting him up. So I brought in a pair of trousers. I was delighted with myself. Handing them to the nun I said, "Is he getting up sister?" I never liked that nun anyway, very cold looking oul' wan.

' "Getting up, of course he's not getting up."

' "I was only wondering because of the clothes."

' "You can take back the trousers—we want the shirt and socks for under the habit." That's what she said, as cool as a cucumber, and without another word walked off.'

'The callous oul' bitch,' a neighbour said. 'May God forgive her. They may be good with the dying but there's the living as well.'

Someone had gone for the death certificate. Once that came the society-man would pay out the policy. My mother cried again when the certificate arrived. Then she looked up from her reading of it and said triumphantly, 'I knew it. He never had TB, look—it's there in black and white—phthisis. That's what ailed him, that's what killed him. No such a thing as TB.'

I wanted to see him. I wanted to see him on my own. No one noticed when I left the house. I walked very slowly to the hospice. Aware as I had been earlier that everyone else was going about their business. No one in the whole world except the family knew or cared that my father was dead. I wanted to think of nothing else and concentrated my mind on his death. Remembering suddenly things I had wanted to ask him, questions to which I'd never now know the answers. I wanted to be consumed by grief but other things intruded. I noticed shop windows and people and found myself smiling at two little boys coaxing an unwilling dog on a length of rope to cross the road. I walked more slowly but eventually came to the big metal gates and began the walk up the drive. Turning now to the left, past the devil's tree and on to the mortuary chapel. I was unprepared for how still he would be. I called his name softly and he didn't answer. He was the only one in the chapel and I was glad of that. I touched him. He was so cold. A long hair curled up from his eyebrow. I kept looking at him, wanting to believe he was only sleeping. That in a minute he would open his eyes and smile at me. Ask me if it was cold outside. I touched his hands and kissed his forehead and with spit on my finger smoothed the unruly eyebrow. I said goodbye to him and walking down the drive was consumed with guilt because suddenly I felt very hungry.

I tried to feel bitterness at all the activity that was going on in the house. Anyone would think my father wasn't lying dead on a slab in the mortuary. Yet despite myself I was caught up in the excitement of buying black which my mother and I would wear, she for a year and me for six months. Money was flowing like water—to pay for stuff for a new dress for me, clothes for my mother, the dyeing of my beautiful heliotrope coat. Death notices in the paper—American and English papers please copy. Telegrams to be sent.

We moved in with my aunt on the day of the funeral. We had roast lamb for dinner—the first joint for years—and the most delicious roast lamb and potatoes I had ever tasted.

I wanted to be sad every minute. Not to be hungry or tired, not to notice all that was going on around me. On the morning of the funeral mass I wanted nothing in my mind but the thought that in a few moments my father's coffin would be taken from here to the cemetery and buried. But the sun was shining through the stained-glass windows and I could hear a bird singing.

The day after the funeral I came home from work and found my mother sitting by the fire. On the table were piles of pound notes and heaps of silver. She was crying and I couldn't help thinking how nice she looked in her new black clothes. She was paler than usual but that suited her too.

'Look,' she said, crying and pointing to the money.

'Look at that. Every undertaker's yard in the city collected for your daddy—he was very well liked. Lord have mercy on him—the comfort I could have given him with half of that. Do you know what I was doing when you came in?'

'No.'

I was crying with her.

'I was just thinking—I have everything. Everything I ever wanted. A house and all that money. Everything I ever wished for. Everything—and I've nothing for I haven't got him.'